Creating Photomontages
with Photoshop

A Designer's Notebook

Creating Photomontages
with Photoshop

PATRICK **COLLANDRE**

DIDIER **CRÉTÉ**

GUILLAUME **DAVEAU**

LAMIA **DHIB**

TAÏ-MARC **LE THANH**

ÉRIC **MAHÉ**

ODILE **PASCAL**

BERNARD **ROSSI**

TRANSLATED BY
WILLIAM **RODARMOR**

O'REILLY®

Beijing • Cambridge • Farnham • Köln • Paris • Sebastopol • Taipei • Tokyo

Creating Photomontages with Photoshop: A Designer's Notebook
by Patrick Collandre, Didier Crété, Guillaume Daveau, Lamia Dhib, Taï-Marc Le Thanh, Éric Mahé, Odile Pascal, and Bernard Rossi

Translated by William Rodarmor

Published by O'Reilly Media, Inc., 1005 Gravenstein Highway North, Sebastopol, CA 95472.

Translation from the French language edition of: *Photomontages créatifs avec Photoshop - Les cahiers des Designers 04* by Patrick Collandre, Didier Crété, Guillaume Daveau, Lamia Dhib, Taï-Marc Le Thanh, Éric Mahé, Odile Pascal, and Bernard Rossi. © 2002 Editions Eyrolles, Paris, France.

O'Reilly books may be purchased for educational, business, or sales promotional use. Online editions are also available for most titles (*safari.oreilly.com*). For more information, contact our corporate/institutional sales department: (800) 998-9938 or *corporate@oreilly.com*.

Editor:	Chuck Toporek
Production Editor:	Darren Kelly
Art Director:	Michele Wetherbee
Cover Designer:	Volume Design, Inc.
Interior Designer:	Anne Kilgore
Printing History:	
January 2005:	First Edition.

ISBN: 0-596-00858-9

[L]

Contents

One thing that made this commission unusual was the visual tags that the company had chosen for its corporate communications. The generic image on the left boldly proclaims that, as the unrivaled leader in its field, Murex stays ahead of the competition. The middle image—the one described in this Studio—refers to so-called exotic products. The one on the right illustrates high-speed packet data transfer. In each case, the image portrays the meaning of the text.

studio 01

PATRICK **COLLANDRE**

Hardware used
- Sinar 4x5 view camera
- Fuji RDP III sheet film
- Nikon F3 35mm camera
- Broncolor and Godard flash units, with tungsten spots
- Xfinity Pro 48 scanner
- Polaroid SprintScan 4000 scanner
- Wacom Intuous2 A3 graphic tablet
- Power Mac G4 - 450 MHz, 1 GB RAM
- 26 and 20 GB hard drives

Software used
- Photoshop 6.0
- Amapi 6.0

Exotic Products

Visual image presented to the client

Quick rendering · Rough with highlights · Final image

The image I chose for this Studio is one of a group of visuals used by Murex, a data-processing company that builds banking software, in its international communications. I was contacted by the creative head of the Aureus agency, which had just won the account. The winning concept called for showing fishes in connected vessels, which would symbolize the various software programs' functions and interactions.

This particular visual was designed to illustrate *exotic banking products*—different and unusual software applications that need to be handled in a particular way. ■

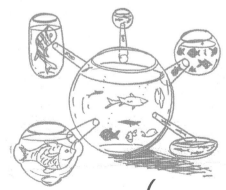

Showing fishes in (**connected vessels would** *symbolize the software programs' various functions and interactions.*

Stage 1

Building a model

Once the general concept was laid out, I had to find a group of shapes that would stress each product's distinctive quality and the smoothness with which information is exchanged between each satellite and the central system. The shapes had to be simple, esthetic, and quite different one from the other.

Plan view

Elevation

After making a few test sketches, I decided to render the transparent glass containers using Amapi software. This allowed me to easily visualize the relationships and dynamic tensions among the shapes.

Rendering the transparent glass containers (with Amapi **allowed me** *to easily visualize the relationship among their shapes*

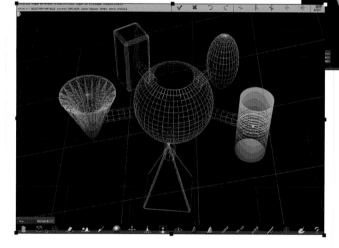

The point of this step was to produce a precise blueprint for a master glassblower who was going to craft the actual aquarium. A quick rendering was all I needed for a presentation to the clients, at which they approved the project. Their only suggestion was that I shorten the glass tubes that radiate like spokes from the center. ■

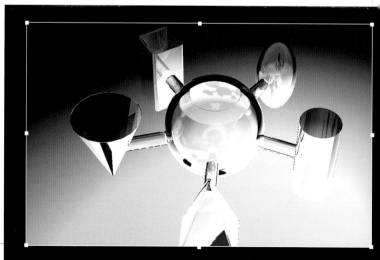

Stage 2

Photographing the fish

This step turned out to be more difficult than I anticipated. I don't own an aquarium, and I soon discovered that photographing fish is a very demanding specialty. Luckily, I was working with an assistant whose uncle ran an exotic fish store, so he knew all about it. The man let me take some photographs in his store, which allowed me to shoot some rare, delicate species.

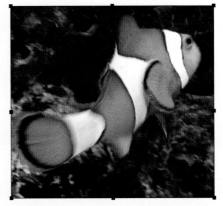

Clown fish, original

Because of the optical (distortions and many reflections, *few of the images were useable.*

Once back in my studio, I started by using my camera to shoot some of the fish in the aquarium built by the master glassblower. But because of the aquarium's many optical distortions and reflections, few of the images were useable. The tank simply had too many different shapes to be photographed in the usual manner.

So I bought a plain, rectangular aquarium, picked up my Nikon, and armed myself with patience. ■

Discus, original

I needed as many pictures of each species as possible—and in various positions—so I would have lots of choices for later creating the montage. I would then overlay the images of the fish onto images of the glass-blown aquarium.

Discus, modified

Stage 3

Photographing the aquarium

This was an all-important stage, as it would determine the quality of the final piece. The glassblower's aquarium was a superb piece of work, but it also embodied every possible problem you can have with light, because of the reflections among its many rounded shapes.

This was an (**all-important stage** that would

determine the quality of the final piece.

I draped the sides of the shooting area with black cloth to avoid reflections. French filmmakers call this "doing a Borniol," a slang expression that comes from Henri de Borniol, a well-known undertaker (who probably used miles of black fabric).

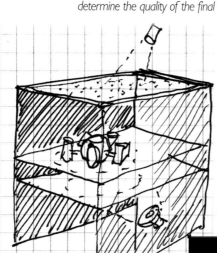

After a couple of tests, it was obvious that I would have to shoot two different pictures: the first showing the aquarium as clearly as possible—without any outside reflections—and the second showing the aquarium with its highlights.

I set the aquarium on a big sheet of rear-projection Plexiglas, with its textured side facing up to avoid producing any additional reflections.

A photograph without outside reflections

I had to create a lighting setup that would bring out the aquarium's shapes and outline its contours. I decided to backlight it, with my main Broncolor light set on the ground, diffused by two layers of translucent Plexiglas.

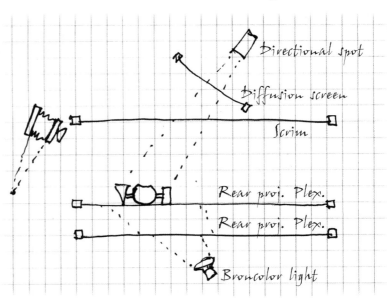

Directional spot

Diffusion screen

Scrim

Rear proj. Plex.

Rear proj. Plex.

Broncolor light

By changing the distance between the two sheets of Plexiglas and the Broncolor unit, I could adjust the light falloff very precisely. The sides of the setup were draped in black velvet.

The "highlights" shot

This shot allowed me to preserve data on highlights and reflections as well as cast shadows. To do this, I placed a spotlight with a Fresnel lens fairly high up in "sunshine" mode—that is, as a single light source—and softened it with a muslin scrim. ∎

Stage 4

Assembling the two aquarium images

When scanned, these two images were exactly alike in size and shape; only the lighting was different.

For starters, I did an overall cleanup, which consisted of simplifying the images to make them easier to work with. I decided to eliminate a few distracting reflections and modify some overly complex gradients.

With the Pen tool I outlined each element and saved it as a path, so I could retrieve it later.

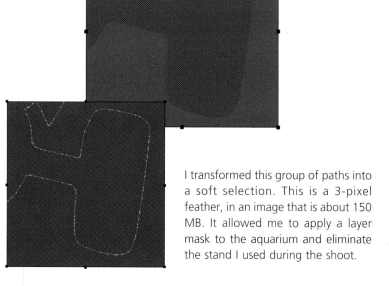

I transformed this group of paths into a soft selection. This is a 3-pixel feather, in an image that is about 150 MB. It allowed me to apply a layer mask to the aquarium and eliminate the stand I used during the shoot.

I then placed the aquarium image on a light gray background, and very carefully aligned the highlighted photograph above it.

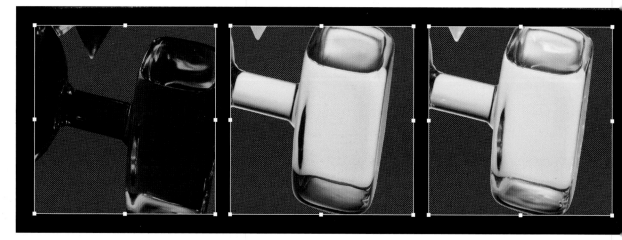

After adjusting the curves, I aligned the upper layer of the "highlighted" image. ■

Stage 5

Adjusting the shadows

Outlining the shadows was tricky and had to be done by hand. In this case I used the Airbrush tool worked in Quick Mask mode. Having a big graphics tablet for tasks like this is very handy.

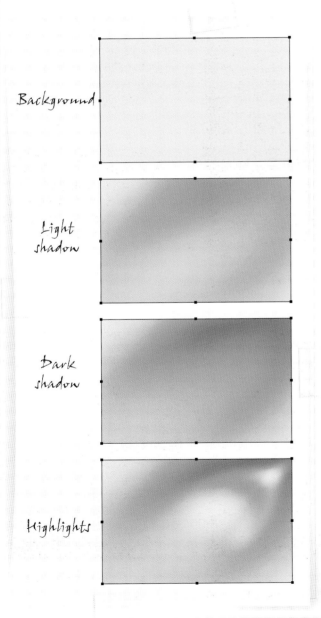

Background

Light shadow

Dark shadow

Highlights

Having roughed out the job, I create a layer mask: a copy of the Highlights layer that I renamed Dark Shadows in Normal mode. I would always be able to modify the gradients so long as I didn't apply the mask to this layer.

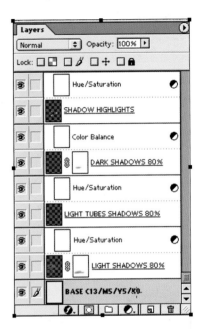

The magnification effects and the (highlights **in the shadows**
could be outlined the same way.

The magnification effects and the highlights in the shadows could be outlined the same way, becoming a new layer named Shadow Highlights in Normal mode (or Screen blending mode).

In photo-realism, shadows are among the trickiest elements to deal with.

In my effort to further simplify the image, I decided to work only with the aquarium's own shadows—in other words, having no shadows under the fish. Now that I've mentioned it, you've probably already noticed this on the final image. But I don't think the lack of those shadows makes the visual any less convincing. ■

Stage 6

Overlaying the fish

Now we come to a very enjoyable step: putting the actors on stage. I chose (and outlined) these lower-order vertebrates according to their position and movements, and placed them in their "space." They had to look natural, both in swimming around their part of the aquarium and in their relationship with their fellow fish. The idea was to suggest that they might be holding discussions, collaborating, glancing around, etc. Our underlying "human" message had to do with work being carried out with good humor and communication.

Once each fish was roughly outlined, I added a layer mask to each layer before using the Airbrush tool to make the merger look convincing. The fins were especially tricky because they're transparent, and you could often still see the fish's original background, which was very different from its new environment. To smooth the transitions, I either changed their values with the Lighten filter and Fade command (depending on the background) or used the Airbrush in Replace Color mode to change their colors.

In a few cases, to get the fish to fit in, I had to hide them under a highlight, putting them behind the "shining glass." This was one advantage of putting the Highlights image in Screen mode.

I simplified the overall visual as much as I could, so viewers would be able to take in the whole picture and grasp it immediately.

When using the (Lasso, it's a good idea to outline *the fish slightly beyond their edges.*

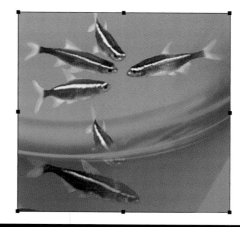

When using the Lasso, it's a good idea to outline the fish slightly beyond their edges. Also, set the Feather to zero to retain some texture. If the fish has a feathered outline, you will lose a few pixels every time you move it. By making a layer mask for each image, you retain all the data until the final placement. ■

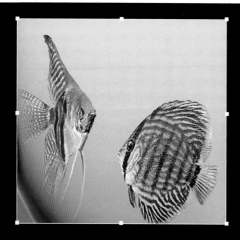  

Now we come to a very enjoyable step: putting the actors on stage. Our underlying "human" message had to do with work being carried out with good humor and communication.

Stage 7

The layers

To help explain how I created the entire montage, I will describe the organization of the different layers. I describe each layer, starting from the bottom and going up stage by stage to the surface (in order words, from the bottom of the page to the top).

Be careful to (name each layer, *otherwise you'll get lost later on.*

First, the Background, a smooth gray layer whose CMYK components I specified. Then the Light Shadows at 80% opacity (I created two shadow layers—light and dark—so I could adjust them separately), and a saturation layer, in almost neutral grays (colors that are even slightly different really stand out).

Next, the gray Light Tubes Shadows at 80%, with a saturation layer, and then the Dark Shadows at 80%, with a Color Balance.

Above that is Shadow Highlights, as we saw in Stage 5, with a Hue/Saturation layer.

We then come to the Aquarium, with three adjustment layers.

Next, the various layers of fish—with their own adjustments, ranging from the Blue-black fish to the Clown fish.

Above that we have Highlights/Aquarium, a layer in Screen mode with its various adjustments. Then Page Layout frame, a useful format for this visual, since our image and its margins will be bigger than the frame.

Then we have the MxCom typography, which contains all of the text used in the final image.

Finally, we come to what I call "the black art." This is a personal trick I discovered by accident that allows me to cut the size of a file when the image is very big. All you have to do is create a Normal layer, fill it with a uniform opaque color, activate it before saving the file, and surprise! You'll notice that the file is now smaller than it originally was. Your results may vary, however, and you will lose the preview image. This trick may be less handy nowadays, when memory is no longer in short supply, but in some circumstances, the savings in disk space can still be considerable. ∎

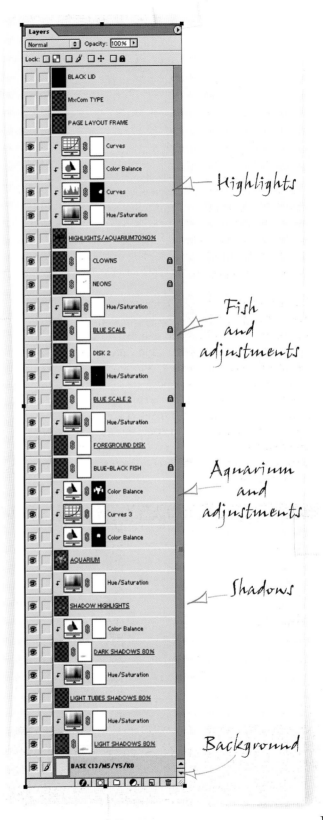

It's great that digital photography lets you change an image as much as you like. What a difference that makes! Now photographers can continue adjusting their pictures long after the shutter clicks.

DIDIER **CRÉTÉ**

Hardware used
- Hasselblad ELX
  Fuji Velvia film
  Broncolor Pulso-spot with Fresnel lens,
  two umbrellas, one spotlight
- JEI drum scanner
- Power Mac G4 - 500 MHz dual processor,
  1 GB RAM

Software used
- Photoshop 6.0
- Flo

A War of Inches

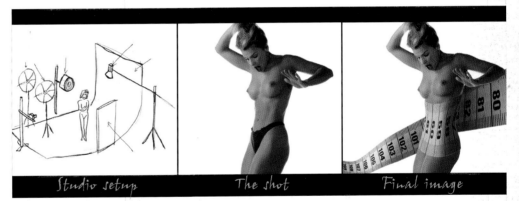

Studio setup   The shot   Final image

I was a little worried about having to illustrate such a well-worn, familiar theme as weight loss, especially since my image was supposed to be neither too stylish nor too scientific. But it still had to be striking, because it would be used for a magazine cover and on posters.

We came up with the idea of a woman looking with surprise at a tape measure wrapped around her waist. All I had to do was find a model who looked convincing, and who was neither too thin nor too fat.

The image was relatively simple and uncluttered, so its entire success depended on the model's expression and the way the tape measure looked around her waist. Even her all-important makeup had to be invisible so she would remain natural and believable.

Everything depended on the model's *(*expression **and the** *way the tape measure looked around her waist.*

Stage 1

Taking the photograph

To bring out the curves on the model's body, I chose fairly strong side lighting. The model, whose name is Stephanie, stood on a seamless white background, far enough away from it to avoid any reflections back onto her skin. The principal light came from a Fresnel maxi on a pole to her left. (This spotlight, which is often used in filmmaking, has a so-called Fresnel lens that lets you modify and focus the light.) To further accentuate the side lighting, we stood a black panel to the model's right. Two umbrellas set at 45-degree angles were added to lighten any overly dark shadows. A spotlight lit up the background nicely; it usually takes a slight

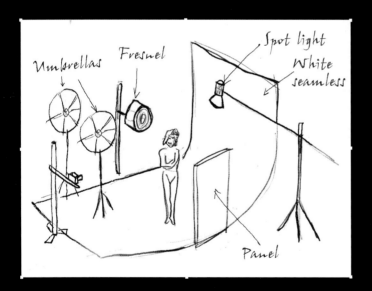

A seamless background is a place in a studio where the wall and the floor meet in a curve, providing an even, shadowless background for the shoot.

overexposure to produce a good clean white.

In this situation, it can be hard for a model to get a sense of the environment and its requirements. So we took a few shots with my assistant holding a white banner around Stephanie's waist.

As we took the pictures, Stephanie gave us a number of satisfactory expressions, but I still felt that a little something was missing. So I asked her to actually shout—and that gave us a lot more realism. Thanks, Stephanie! ■

Stage 2

Color balance

It is extremely important that your computer setup be properly calibrated. For Mac users, ColorSync is invaluable for this; it lets you set up your system's default color profile. My monitors and scanner have their own profiles (they're like color balance ID cards), so I can be sure I'm working with the right colors.

The raw scanner image accurately reflected the fact that the processed slide was a little dark and had a slightly warm cast, which is typical of Velvia film.

The raw scanner image

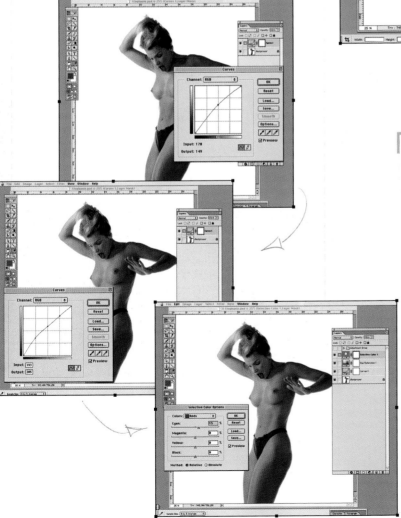

Photoshop's Adjustment Layers deserve a lot of praise. They're extremely adaptable and don't increase file size. In addition, they let you change or undo color balance retouching steps whenever you like.

In Photoshop, I prefer to use a Curves adjustment layer for color balance corrections. I started by just raising the midtones to lighten the image. There was no need to touch the black or white tones, since they were set during the scan.

The dark colors looked too dense, so we went back to Curves and raised them. The light colors were fine, so it was a good idea to protect them by using points.

To fix the overall reddish cast, I used the Curves layer and Image→Adjustments→Selective Color. ■

19

Stage 3

The cleanup

In spite of appearances, a scanned white is never one hundred percent white. You can check this with the Eyedropper Tool and the information palette. Beware of dirty whites when it's time to print the image!

Take the Lasso tool and do a rough outline of the subject, invert it, and fill it with white.

The area around the model was cleaned with the Dodge Tool set in a gamut of light colors at 20%. That way, I was sure to get a white background while avoiding a harsh outline.

> If you're not careful, the Clone Stamp Tool will quickly produce a mosaic effect as it copies material. To avoid that, be sure to frequently change the sample source.

To deal with the shadows under the model's head, the best choice was our old friend, the Clone Stamp Tool. For safety, I prefer to make a selection of the zones I want to protect. Beyond that, it's up to you. But remember: if you set the opacity too low you'll get blurring; if you set it too high you'll get marbling.

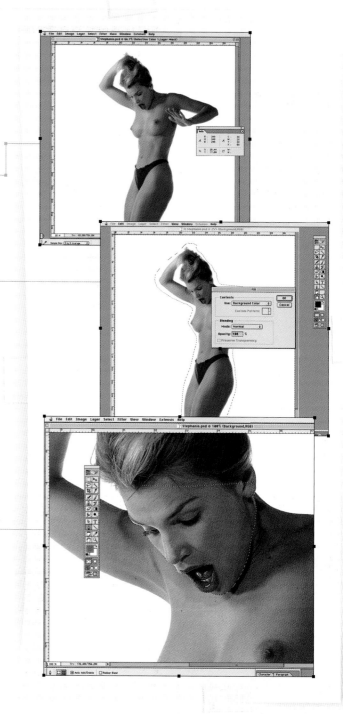

When people saw the resulting image, everybody thought the model's thighs were a little heavy. All right, all right!—I think they were making too big a deal of it, though. So I made a quick selection, copied Stephanie's thighs onto a layer, and reshaped them by hand, slimming the lower part. That was better. And I further refined her legs with the Liquefy filter. Whew! ∎

Stage 4

Positioning the tape measure

When we shot the measuring tape, it was vital that we used consistent lighting. In fact, we tried to match the light we used with Stephanie exactly. But we had to rely on trial and error to give the measuring tape the desired shape, since there was no way to actually line it up in advance.

The Pen is one of the most efficient outlining tools, so I used it to outline the measuring tape. I turned the path into a selection, then slid and pasted it onto the picture of Stephanie to see how things looked.

Be sure to zoom in and out often, which is why having a fast graphics tablet is important.

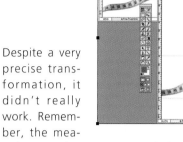

Despite a very precise transformation, it didn't really work. Remember, the measuring tape has to wrap precisely around the model's waist. The middle segment of the tape is crucial—it determines the rest of the montage. We therefore divided the measuring tape into three parts.

We outlined the middle portion of the tape, cut and pasted it to create a layer we called "Tape measure middle," and then transformed it manually.

In Photoshop, you can name layers and group them in a folder. It's worth taking advantage of this, because layers in a photomontage multiply very fast and can quickly be hard to find.

The left and right segments of the tape measure were already outlined, so we used the Lasso Tool to split them. Because these parts had to go behind Stephanie's body, we created a path around her hips. We named this path and kept it nice and warm, because we would use it a few more times later on. We created a selection of this path and applied a layer mask to one of the two layers in question. All we had to do was repeat the operation on the other layer. The tape measure now encircled her body nicely. ■

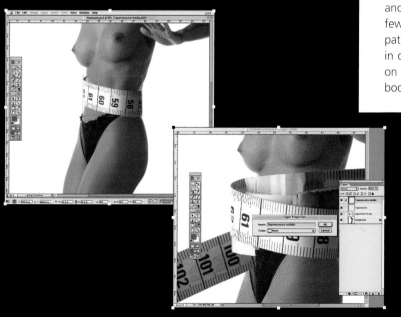

Stage 5

Transforming the measuring tape

At this point, some people might say, "That's fine, Didier. The girl's beautiful, the measuring tape is around her waist—everything's great!" But I didn't think we were quite done yet. So we decided to be a little more daring. The measuring tape just sort of sat there; we fiddled with it a bit to really cinch it tight.

As in Stage 4, we started with the middle segment of the tape measure and used the Edit→Transform→Distort command to stretch the tape so that it covered Stephanie's entire torso. Now we could refine the image by erasing the parts we didn't want.

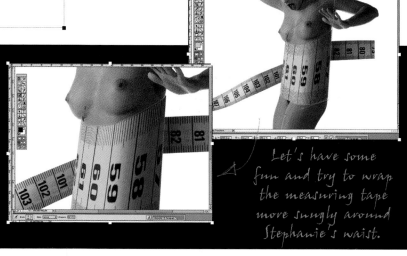

Let's have some fun and try to wrap the measuring tape more snugly around Stephanie's waist.

At the time I did this photomontage I used a dedicated distortion program called Flo to reshape the measuring tape. It has a number of useful tools, and I still like it.

That software is no longer available, however, so let's create the distortion with Photoshop's Liquefy filter. The results shouldn't be too bad. Come on—don't give up! I'm sure you'll get the distortion effect you want after a few million attempts. It helps to bring the torso layer forward from time to time; that will give you a good look at the parts that still remain to be reshaped.

To finish, all you have to do is to eliminate the parts that stick out, such as the edges of her panties. But rather than erase them, I prefer to paint those parts in white on a separate layer. That way, you leave the base photo untouched—you never know. ■

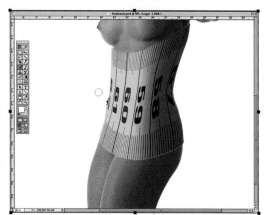

Stage 6

The finishing touches

We now had to deal with the two other segments of the measuring tape, which were still ridiculously small. First we copied the measuring tape layer and really changed its shape, to give it some impact. Rats!—now it was covering the model's arm!

Here's a trick: To get a mask of an active selection, just hold the Option key down and click on the little mask icon at the bottom of the Layers palette.

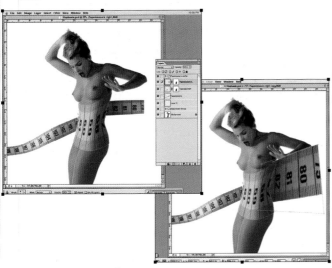

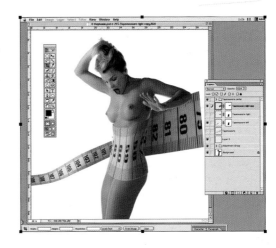

When you do big transformations, it's (wise *to work on a copy of the layer.*

So we carefully outlined the arm (using the Pen, of course) and created a layer mask.

We were able to do the same transformation to the left side of the measuring tape without any problem. And there we are—all done!

The next day, however, I looked at the picture before I delivered it, and I thought the measuring tape seemed a little dark. If I could, I would have put the three layers that comprise the tape segments in a single folder and used an adjustment layer (a Curve) on it. Alas, an adjustment layer can't be applied to all of the layers in a folder, but that shortcoming was corrected in Photoshop 7, so all you folks with CS should try this out.

Instead, I applied the same Curve to the three layers in question. Luckily there were only three of them, and not one hundred! ■

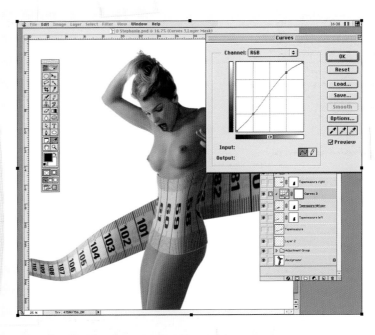

Compared to old-fashioned film methods, graphic software has caused a revolution in the way we manipulate images in special effects and photomontages. In recent years, digital photography has proved a valuable creative part of that process. It's instantaneous, precise, and flexible, all of which changes our approach and reveals new fields of expressive possibilities. So let your creativity soar!

studio 03

GUILLAUME **DAVEAU**

Taking Flight

Hardware used
- Nikon D1 for location shots
- Hasselblad with Leaf back for studio shots
- Power Mac G4 - 450 MHz dual processor, 1 GB RAM

Software used
- Photoshop 6.0
- Leaf Capture utility

Joining the images   The working model   Final image

As a personal project, I wanted to create an image of clothing flying through the air. My first thought was to have the clothes whirling above a front-loading washing machine in a laundromat, and make their motion visible.

Before Photoshop and digital cameras came along, I used to create special effects during the photo shoot itself, a specialty that made use of everything from the most wonderful optical effects to the cheesiest of tricks. And any items that had to defy the laws of gravity wound up on huge, heavy, very sharp sheets of glass.

So when digital became practical, I dove headlong into the sea of pixels, ditching the sheets of glass as I moved toward new special effects where shooting the photograph digitally quickly became unbeatable.

I think the clothes in this image are a (good illustration *of what I mean.*

Stage 1

Scouting the locale

It took me two evenings of scouting to find a laundromat that looked right. Its row of washing machines gave a strong sense of perspective, which was further strengthened by the converging lines of the floor tiles.

Adding spice to the shoot was the fact that I couldn't get very far away from the machines. In most of today's professional SLR cameras, the image chip covers an effective area of 18 × 24 mm. Optically, this means that a 24mm lens is actually a 35mm one (more or less). Glancing through the viewfinder, I figured approximately how I would put the picture together, in terms of framing, the clothes' flight path, and how I would position them.

Because of the practical limitation I mentioned earlier, I had to take three panoramic photographs and join them together, which wound up making the useable image bigger.

Glancing through the viewfinder, *(I figured approximately how I would put the picture together.*

The pictures were taken on a perfectly level plane, but without centering each image on the lens's optical center. This produced images that were easy to connect. The visual setup was simple enough that it was faster to join the image layers in Photoshop, working on associated masks, and retouching any little defects with the Clone Stamp Tool. ■

Stage 2

The clothes

The clothes are the principal actors, so we have to treat them with special care if we want the montage to be dynamic and believable.

They should appear to be taking off on their own, with the yellow shirt sneaking out of the washing machine, the violet one soaring, the pants floating in midair, and the blue jacket taking flight.

Helping the clothes express themselves fully required a slew of tissue paper, sheets of polystyrene, pins, and a host of other tiny articles and tricks.

Working on a horizontal surface, I stuffed tissue paper into the yellow and purple shirts to give them shape and make them look as if they were flying.

Because I was working on different planes, and the images were going to be slightly rotated when they were placed on the picture of the laundromat (see Stage 3), it was important to keep an eye on the direction and character of the lighting— I needed the light to appear as if it were coming from the neon ceiling lights.

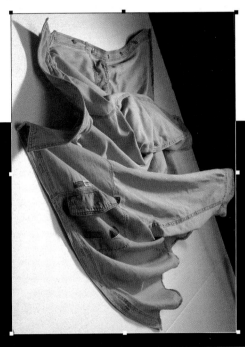

The blue jacket and the shirt in the foreground, on the other hand, were hung and shaped while on a vertical surface. I wanted to accentuate their curves and give them an impression of floating and fluidity.

Here, digital photography is a real (ace in the hole **in the** *service of creativity.*

Here, digital photography turns out to be a real ace in the hole in the service of creativity. The picture is available immediately, and you can see it on screen instead of shooting a test Polaroid or waiting for a film proof. You can do a sample montage very quickly, and reshoot to your heart's content to refine the photograph. What a difference software makes compared to doing special effects the old way! ■

Stage 3

Placing the clothes on the background image and integrating the layers

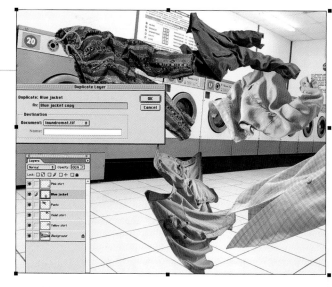

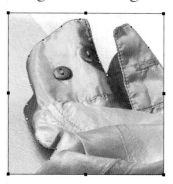

I retouched each clothing image with the Clone Stamp Tool, outlined it with the Pen Tool, and integrated it as an individual layer with the picture of the laundromat —while respecting the order of the overlaps, of course. It's very important to carefully name the layers, and stick to your system religiously.

To establish the position and exact size of each article of clothing, I made a duplicate of each layer so that I could work on a model of the picture.

Many operations (including transformations) slightly degrade the data because of rounding during algorithm calculations, and it's important to avoid having these add up. On the other hand, you can manipulate the layers of a model as much as you like, and then apply a single transformation to each final image layer at the end.

It's very important to (carefully name **the layers, and** *stick to your system religiously.*

When the layers were added (by cut and paste or drag and drop) to the image, they came in with perfectly sharp edges, whether the clothes were near or far, and even when they were supposed to be moving.

So I had to blur their edges to adapt them to the image, but not in a uniform way. I applied the blur selectively, depending on local contrasts and the different details between the edge of the clothing and the laundromat picture.

A strong local contrast— blue on white, say, as opposed to blue on gray— adds to an edge's apparent sharpness, and requires more blurring.

I then retrieved the transparent layer selection and linked it to a mask to which I applied a Gaussian Blur, with a radius of 1.5 pixels. This adjustment is made on a case-by-case basis, depending on the texture of the clothing and its position in space. You can also shrink the selection slightly before creating the mask. This has the effect of further masking the edges of the clothes while maintaining the intensity of the blur.

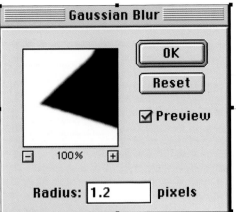

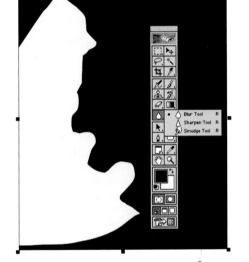

In specific areas, I refined the edges of the mask using two pairs of tools: Blur/Sharpen and Pen (or Airbrush)/Eraser, with an average opacity of 30% to 50%.

A mask can be modified indefinitely without altering the image, so feel free to change it to your heart's content.

When checking effects, always set the view to 100%.

A mask can be modified indefinitely (without altering the image, so feel free *to change it to your heart's content.*

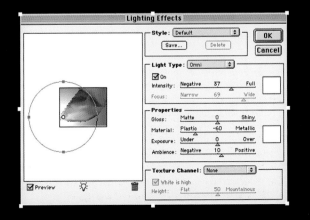

An energetic washing machine drum

Since the clothes had to look as if they were shooting out of the washing machine's drum before taking flight, the image would be strengthened if the drum itself provided a feeling of motion.

This is the idea behind the streaks, but we accented it with the Lighting Effects filter to add some glow to the yellow shirttail that is still in the washing machine. ■

Stage 4

The streaks

To explain how the streaks in the picture are created, I'll use the blue jacket as an example. We start by going to the model, retrieving the pathway of the streaks, and dragging and dropping its icon onto the visual. We then adapt it to the picture by scaling the activated path. This serves as a placement guide.

We then duplicate the jacket layer as a jacket streak layer, and move it toward the center of the area it is supposed to cover, applying a Motion Blur with an angle of 5 degrees and a distance of 320 pixels.

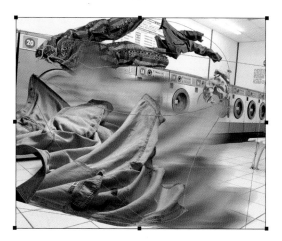

Each layer requires its own adjustments, of course, and will be scaled up or down so it covers its designated location.

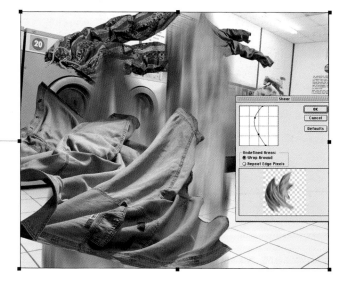

In order to make the streak curve around, we use the Filter→Distort→Shear filter. This filter only works on a vertical axis, so we start by rotating the layer 90 degrees clockwise (Image→Rotate Canvas→90° CW).

We then adjust the Shear filter using anchoring points, depending on how much of an effect we want, which is hard to judge from the Preview. Finally, we rotate the layer 90 degrees counterclockwise (Image→Rotate Canvas→90° CCW) to bring it back where it belongs.

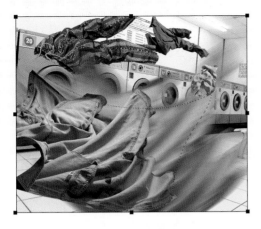

Adding shadows

To give the rendering some modeling, we're going to use the Airbrush to paint shadows on a new layer with black set to 70%, using a preset with soft edges, a wide diameter (100-300 pixels), and light opacity (10-30%).

It's important to execute this stage carefully, because shadows are the foundation of a successful visual image. In our case, the light is coming from the ceiling's neon lights, so the shadows on horizontal surfaces will be much darker than the ones on vertical surfaces.

To finish up, we refine the opacity of the shadows layer. The shadows are now present, discreetly giving the picture a feeling of depth. ■

It's important to execute (this stage, **carefully because shadows** *are the foundation of a successful visual image.*

We then retrieve the selected streak path, apply a 50-pixel feather to it, and create a mask associated with the blue streak layer.

To finish, we adjust the layer's opacity to the desired intensity and clean up the mask's edges with the Pen or Eraser tools at a fairly light opacity (10-30%), depending on the degree of transparency desired, and erase any areas in the streak that show through too strongly.

We could also slightly combine the effect of the streak with the jacket, by treating the jacket mask the same way.

All that remains to be done is to repeat the same operation for each item of clothing before moving on to the final stage.

Parfum d Orient

You are plunged into the intoxicating warmth
of an Oriental night. As the moon hides its charms,
other charms are being unveiled . . .

studio 04

LAMIA **DHIB**

The Perfume Woman

Hardware used
- Nikon Coolpix 800 with digital zoom
- Power Mac 6500 - 528 MB RAM, 6 GB hard drive

Software used
- Photoshop 6.0

Initial photograph   *Perfume bottle*   *Final image*

I have occasionally produced advertising visuals for beauty products by Clarins and Mugler, so I was immediately drawn to the idea of creating a photomontage to promote a new perfume with an Oriental fragrance. Beyond the perfume bottle—which I obviously had to show—I could give my imagination free rein in choosing the setting for the photograph. I quickly settled on the languid mood of the *Thousand and One Nights* story, building the image around a photograph of a naked woman glimpsed within the bottle, gazing at a starry Oriental night. Given femininity, sensuality, and a perfumed night, the project was launched. ■

I quickly settled on the (**languid** mood of the
Thousand and One Nights *story in building the image.*

Stage 1

Taking the picture

I shot the photograph in the simplest possible way. I asked my model, Sophie, to sit on a stool near my window, and I drew the curtains; I didn't want any onlookers, since Sophie was completely naked. For lighting I just used my desktop lamp. Before starting to take pictures, we carefully removed everything within the camera's field of view, so as to reduce the amount of touch-up I would have to do to the final image. I'm not a professional photographer, so I used my digital camera and just began taking pictures. Sophie had to strike several poses before I got a good shot.

The shot

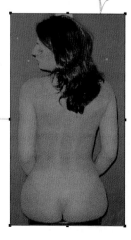

Cropping

I then cropped the photograph in Photoshop, keeping only the part I wanted. The Crop Tool is in the palette in the left part of the screen.

The cropped image

For a photo shoot, it's a good idea to use a neutral-colored background; it makes outlining and masking the image easier. In this case, the background is blue because those were the curtains in my room. If necessary, you can always use a white sheet.

After cropping, our image is now smaller—but don't worry. This stage allows us to shrink the image's file size. ■

Stage 2

Color balance

The task now was to colorize our model before putting her into the bottle, to suggest the mood of the final image. Since the atmosphere will be that of an Oriental night, I chose to use shades of blue.

In the Image menu, choose Mode→Grayscale and click OK, and, while still in the Image menu, select Mode→Duotone mode. Once in the Duotone window, activate the Tritone window.

I retained the (**shadowing** on my model's shoulder and hip, *so the final rendering would have some relief.*

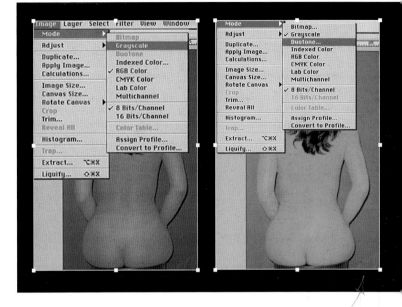

Duotone mode is grayed out.

By default, the first color is black and the two others are white. To fill in these two colors, click in the white square next to Ink 2. The Custom Colors dialog box opens, in which you can choose the color you want. In this case I chose Pantone Blue 072 CVC. Do the same for the third color.

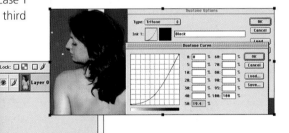

To modify the curve of the black color, click in the Ink 1 color square. A window opens, in which you can adjust the curve. I chose to lower the intensity of the black on the left side of my model. This lets me retain the shadowing on Sophie's shoulder and hip, so the final rendering will have some relief. It also improves the way she looks inside the perfume bottle. ∎

Important: You must start with the Grayscale option; otherwise you won't be able to open the Duotone window to apply the Tritone to the image.

Stage 3

The gradation

On a new layer, I created a gradient from dark to light blue, and set the layer in Multiply mode at 75% opacity. Using the Tools palette, I made the foreground color dark blue and the background light blue.

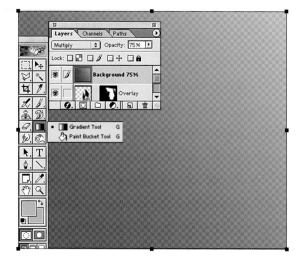

Be cautious when experimenting with values. If you add too much brightness and contrast, you can lose some of the picture's texture.

Then I recreated the gradient in the same direction on a new layer. I set the layer in Overlay mode and placed it above the first gradient. I selected the Background (the second gradient), brought in my visual (the perfume bottle), and pasted it. I then set the Bottle layer in Overlay mode at 100% opacity. ■

I then took the following steps to give my perfume bottle some volume. I first created a path of the bottle with the Pen tool, and saved my selection. In the Image menu I went to Adjustments→Brightness/Contrast. When the dialog opened, I typed in the values that felt most appropriate: Brightness +21 and Contrast +13.

Stage 4

The model

Now we will retrieve the Bottle selection with the Select➤Reselect command, get the image of the model, select it, and quit the document. We are now in the Bottle layer. Select the model and use the Edit➤Paste Into command to put her in the bottle. By doing this, you will have created a layer mask. The layer mask has two thumbnails: the image and a black square. You will now be working in the black square, which corresponds to the mask. The Model layer will be placed above the Bottle layer in Normal mode at 100% opacity.

We now enter the trickiest, but most interesting stage. Be sure to name your layers carefully so you can keep track of them.

Look for a square with a selected circle next to the small eye. This means that you are in the layer mask thumbnail.

It's very important that you be in the layer mask thumbnail when getting ready to erase. If you are in the Model thumbnail instead, you might actually erase the image and make it disappear.

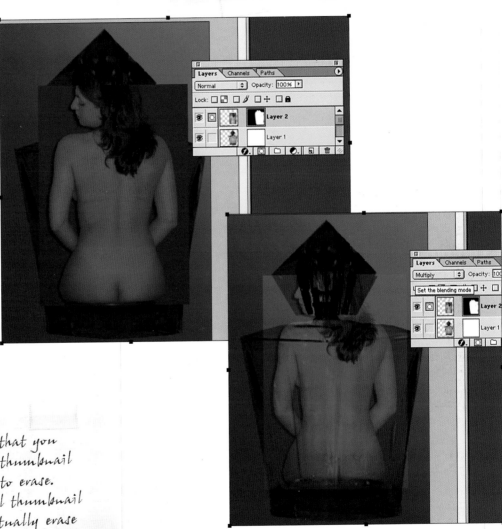

Now set your layer in Overlay mode with 100% opacity. You will be able to erase the parts you want to get rid of while seeing the outline of the bottle, which helps you as you work. ■

Stage 5

Erasing

Take the Eraser Tool, go to the toolbar, and pick the Airbrush option with a blur shape of 300 pixels and 100% opacity. Start erasing the parts of the image you don't need. Mask the layers that are in your way during this operation, and choose a fairly small preset to work in tricky areas. You can also reduce the opacity for different parts of the picture. For example, I chose an opacity of 100% on the upper part of Sophie's body, 60% for her left side, and 90% for her right. ▪

Be careful (not to confuse

"Paste" with "Paste Into."

In your Tool palette put the black in the foreground and the white in the background. The black will erase, whereas the white causes the image to disappear.

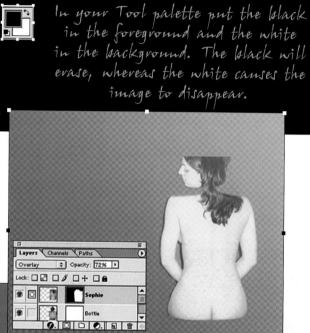

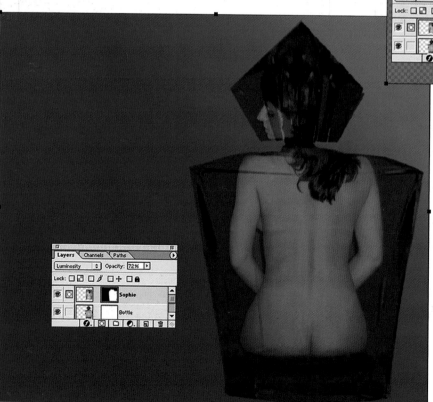

Be careful not to confuse "Paste" with "Paste Into." Paste will create a new layer which overlays the bottle. Paste Into will put the layer in the bottle, which allows you to create the layer mask.

Stage 6

The moon

What would an Oriental night be without the moon or stars?

Rather than drawing a moon myself, I went on the Internet, where I found a picture of a moon with some clouds in the foreground (obviously). Select the moon, then close its window. Return to the Background layer and select Edit→Paste Into. Set the moon layer in Hard Light with 81% opacity and place it above the original background layer (the gradient). Make the clouds disappear by erasing them, using the same procedure as in Stage 5.

If you can draw well, I urge you to use Illustrator to create your moon. Illustrator will produce a better rendering than Photoshop can, and your moon will have roundness and a distinct curve. Another approach is to scan the drawing of a moon from a book. Or else you can do as I did, and find the moon on the Web.

First moon in Hard Light mode

Second moon in Lighten mode

I originally tried using just one moon, but it was too dark, and didn't come across very well.

In order to get a nice shiny moon, I suggest you add a second one by repeating the operation. Keep the clouds, set the Moon 2 layer in Lighten mode at 100%. Place it above the first one and superimpose the two to produce a single moon. ■

Stage 7

The stars

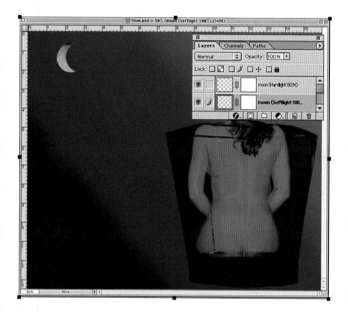

You can also produce beautiful stars with Illustrator. Try it!

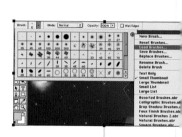

The preset menu is found in the Window→Tool Presets menu. To load a preset, just go to the pull-down menu of the Option bar and select Load Tool Presets. A window opens from which you can select a tool preset and load it.

Now create a new layer in Normal mode 100% and choose a preset (for the Pencil, Brush, Airbrush, etc.). From the preset forms I chose the Crosshatch brush (Edit→Preset Manager→Brushes) and used it to dot the sky with stars. Pressing and holding on the preset produces bigger stars

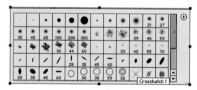

To make a star shine more brightly, pick a round preset—you'll find them on the preset palette—zoom into a star, and apply the round preset in the middle.

Here is another way to create a starry sky. First, fill a layer with a gradient from bottom to top, choosing dark blue for the foreground and white for the background. Create a second layer, go to the Filter menu, apply the Render→Clouds filter, and set the layer in Multiply mode. In the Filter menu, apply the Render→Lens Flare effect to the layer and repeat the operation several times. Be careful to adjust the Lens Flare's brightness so you get a uniform sky. (In the Lens Flare window, you can move the light source to where you want it to appear in the image.) Then choose the Brush Tool. Put the white color in the foreground and paint dots all over your image. In the Filter menu, apply a very slight Gaussian Blur to the layer and add a little brightness and contrast (by going to Image→Adjustments→Brightness/Contrast). When you merge your two sky layers, the result will be a beautiful starry sky! ■

Stage 8

Adding the text

Select your text and click OK. By default, a layer will be placed above the others. Keep it in Normal mode with 100% opacity.

In the Layers palette, go to the Layer Style window and click the options you want to use. Here I used Bevel and Emboss in Overlay mode with white for the light colors, and Multiply mode with white at 100% for the shadow areas. Click the Satin, Drop Shadow (set to a -40 degree angle) and the Inner Glow boxes, then click OK.

> There are two ways to bring up the Layer Style window: you can double-click your layer's thumbnail, or find the Layer menu and choose Layer Properties.

In the Layer Style window, you will find a wide variety of transformations and effects that you can apply to your text. Don't be afraid to try out different filters, different angles, etc.; you will certainly find something that suits you. Have fun, but don't go overboard with effects if you want a professional-looking result.

Then apply a Gaussian Blur at 1.5 pixels and click OK. Set your layer in Screen blending mode at 100% and click OK again.

Once the effects are applied, click OK and set your text layer in Multiply mode at 100% opacity. It's up to you to try different modes to see which one suits your background better. For the typography, I chose Civitype, a very elegant, Oriental-style font. ■

Apply a Gaussian Blur . . .

. . .and set in Multiply mode.

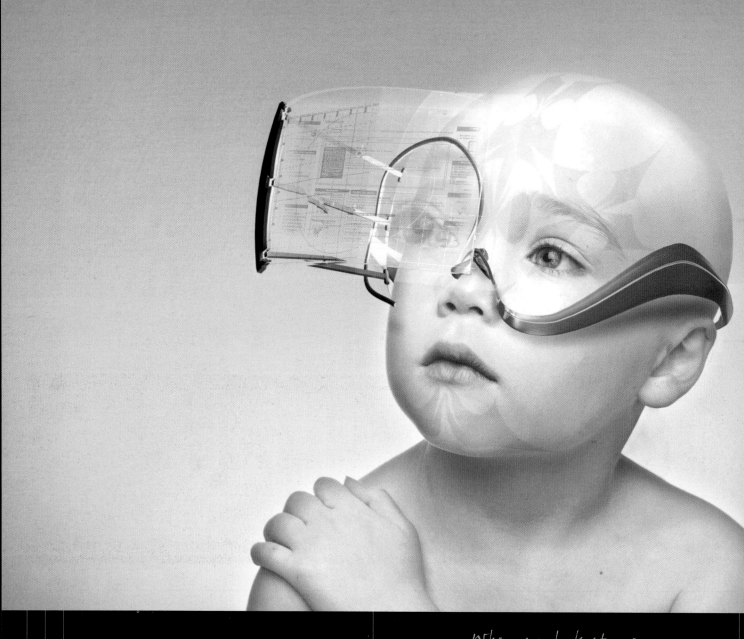

When you look at one
of your finished projects, do you ever feel
there's a gap between the result and what you
had originally imagined? You can close that
gap by deepening your knowledge of the digital
graphic tools available today. You can also
choose to deliberately move away from your
initial concept and embrace the possibilities
offered by various programs. Either way,
remember that these applications are merely
tools in the service of your imagination.

studio 05

TAÏ-MARC LE THANH

The High-Tech Child

Hardware used

- Pentax 6 × 7 camera
- Agfa RSX II 50 film
- Flash unit, softbox
- Epson Expression 1600 Pro scanner
- Power Mac G4 - 450 MHz dual processor, 512 MB RAM 27 GB hard drive

Software used

- Photoshop 6.0
- Illustrator 9.0
- Cinema 4D 7.0

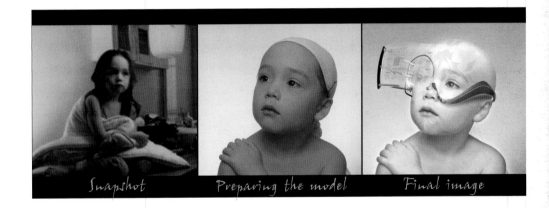

Snapshot   Preparing the model   Final image

The plan for this project was to create a picture of a "high-tech" child wearing a pair of futuristic glasses, with a Web site splash page projected onto one of the lenses. In retouching the photograph of the girl, I first had to make her bald, then tattoo her; I also had to lighten her skin. The image raised two main problems: when people see a pale, bald child, they immediately think of illness; and the futuristic look had to be convincing, because the line between high tech and kitsch is a very fine one.

There were two main stages of the project: retouching the photograph itself, and integrating the outside elements.

Taking photographs of a (child has its own special requirements.

You have to be quick, because children get restless, and you must get written permission from both parents.

43

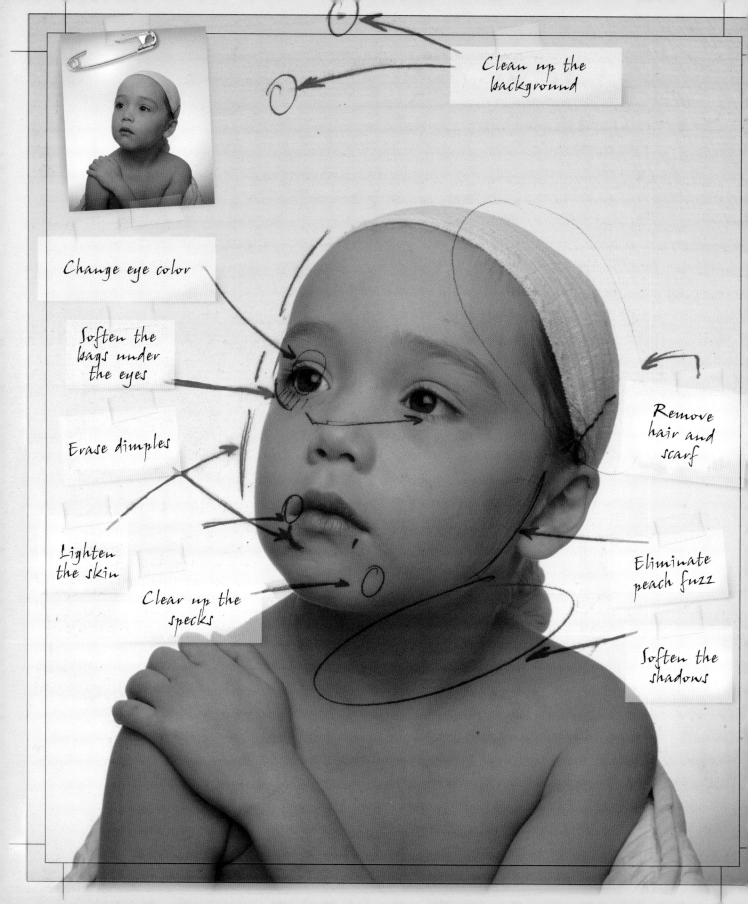

Stage 1

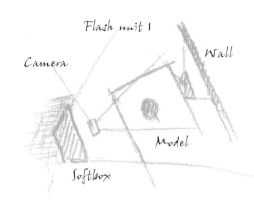

Taking the picture

I started by establishing the overall lighting. To get the picture I needed—namely, a very pale face in a photo with hardly any contrast—I chose lighting that would produce few shadows. I set a softbox directly in front of the girl, and a flash unit to light the white wall behind her (see the sketch). In addition, I used a little makeup, because when you lighten a model's skin color you can't avoid lightening everything else. For this reason, we used mascara on the girl's eyes. I could also have reduced the contrast on her face with some light foundation makeup, or even face powder. The girl in the final image would be bald, so we put a scarf on the model's head to keep her hair from being visible, while showing the shape of her skull.

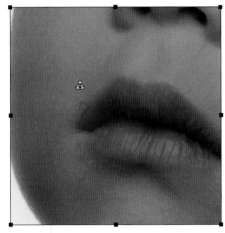

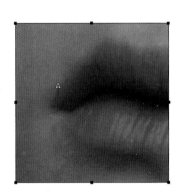

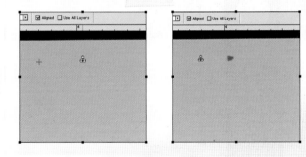

The dust on the girl's lip was trickier because it straddled two areas of different tonality. The size of the Clone Stamp had to be adjusted appropriately (in other words made fairly small), and its opacity lowered even further (to 30%). I also varied the sample areas. For the top part of the dust spot, I took samples from the upper part of the lip; for the bottom, from the lip itself. ■

Cleaning up the spots

The initial retouching of the photograph involved cleaning up some specks. How hard this was depended on where they were. For the spots on the blue background, you can just use the Clone Stamp Tool while copying a zone of the same color. Zoom in and out as you work, and be sure to enlarge the view to life-size, regularly checking your progress. To produce a more gradated effect, don't set the Clone Stamp's opacity to the maximum. Here, it was only at 60%.

The problem with the Clone Stamp is that people often use it too quickly. They fall into the trap of filling up the History palette, and then find they can't backup to undo steps. Also, it's smart to zoom in and out to check your progress.

S t a g e 2

The peach fuzz

The rest of the retouching work involved more specific operations. To remove the peach fuzz on the girl's cheek, I used the Clone Stamp, sampling first from areas to the right of her chin, then moving gradually along the edge of her cheek. The Clone Stamp's opacity was set at 15% and its size at 45. Don't forget to use the Zoom Tool to go in and out between different views.

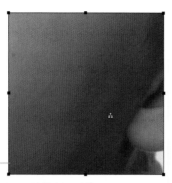

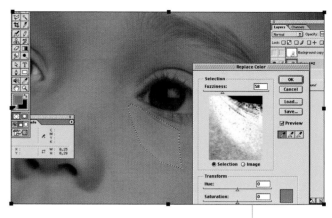

Bags under the eyes

I first selected the bag under the eye with the Lasso and applied a feather of about 30 pixels. I selected an area of somewhat dark skin using the Eyedropper, then used Replace Color to lighten it. That way, the bag disappeared but the skin texture remained.

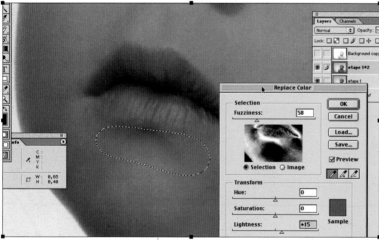

The neck's shadow

I proceeded the same way as for the bags under the eyes, while taking care to use the Lasso to select a large area of the neck and the right cheek. I used a fairly light sample when modifying the color.

The dimple under the lower lip

This operation combined the two preceding ones: a slight Replace Color, followed by using the Clone Stamp, while retaining consistency in the shadows.

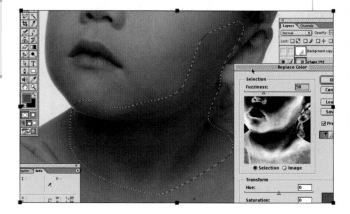

By this stage, we had already made some noticeable changes to the image. The main difficulty would be in preserving the picture's grain and texture while maintaining its overall brightness. ▪

Before

After

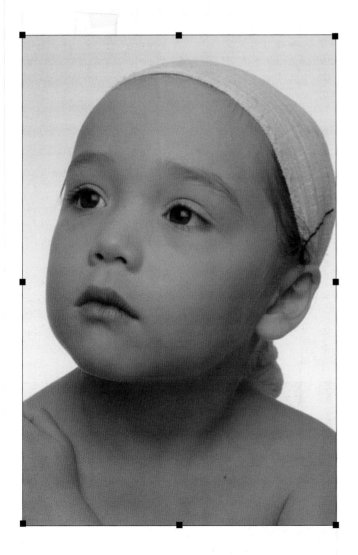

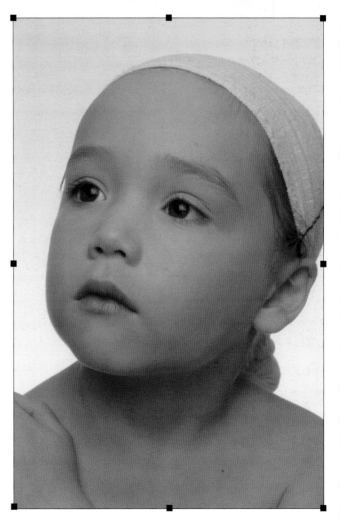

Stage 3

The skull

First, I used the Lasso to determine the general shape of the skull, following the outline of the scarf. This selection was copied to a new layer. Then, starting from the base image, I copied parts of the cheek, forehead, etc., which became different "skin texture" layers. The next step was to reconnect all of these fragments in order to mask the scarf area with bare skin. I used the Eraser to connect them, while softening their outlines. Once that was done, I merged the different fragment layers and used the Clone Stamp, too,l on all layers to refine the skull's general appearance, including the place where it meets the ear.

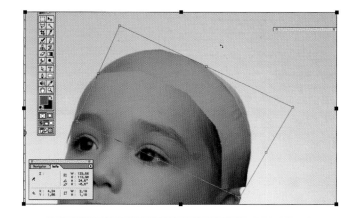

I was careful not to merge the layer with the overall skull shape layer. That one serves as a template and must be on its own layer, so the shape can be retrieved whenever it's needed.

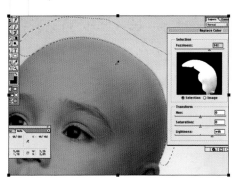

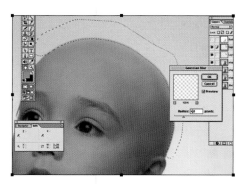

Shaping the skull is complete.

Using the Replace Color function, I corrected the lighting and color balance on certain areas of the skull—the shadow on the temple, the light on the forehead and parietal bones, etc.

Executing these operations while keeping the lighting consistent required some drawing skill; don't be afraid to refer to anatomical diagrams. Once the shaping of the skull was finished, the trick was to integrate it with the background. I selected the edge of the skull with the Lasso and used Replace Color to create the thin line of light reflected off the illuminated wall.

I also applied a very slight Gaussian Blur so the outline wouldn't be too sharp. To finish up, I used the Clone Stamp to eliminate the strand of hair sticking out next to the girl's left eye, and erased the scarf knot at her neck, on the right. ■

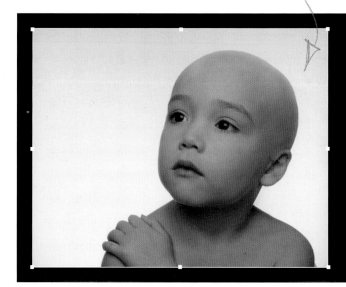

S t a g e 4

Lightening the skin

The difficulty of this stage lies in preserving the texture of the skin while reducing its brightness and contrast. The dominant elements of the face—the eyes, nose, and mouth—must remain identical to the original image, so I selected and copy-pasted them to a new layer.

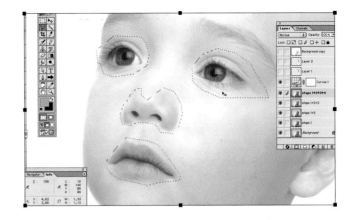

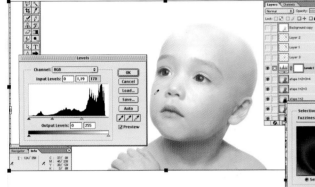

To lighten the face, I gave the image a Levels adjustment layer, which let me simultaneously increase brightness and contrast, while preserving the skin texture.

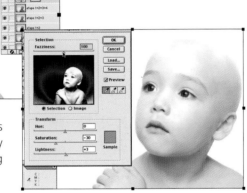

This last step may bring out some undesirable shadow areas. They actually come from the various manipulations in Stage 2, and must be remedied with the techniques from that stage.

This stage is relatively delicate. If you let the colors get too light, the photograph will look underdeveloped. Also, you risk permanently losing skin texture and grain.

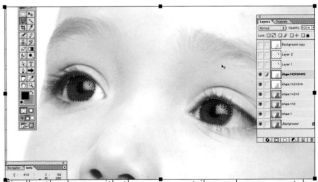

Finally, the layer with the eyes, nostrils, and nose must be integrated with the image. Here I changed it from Normal to Overlay mode at 40%. The approximate outlining of the elements will blend with the image, and the darker areas will accent the eyes, nose, and mouth. ∎

Stage 5

The color of the eyes

We will now use a separate layer to change the color and brightness of the eyes. This allows for more flexibility in color balance manipulations without affecting the face's overall appearance.

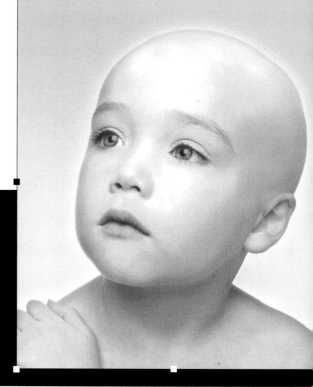

First, I selected the pupil, but not the small, square catch-light in each eye. Otherwise, when we later change the color of the eyes, the catch-light would also change and may turn an unsightly color. I then did a 2-pixel feather selection—which allowed the eye layer to blend more smoothly into the face—and created a new layer with the pupil, in Dodge mode.

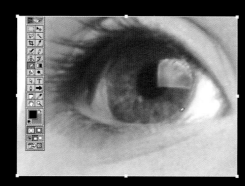

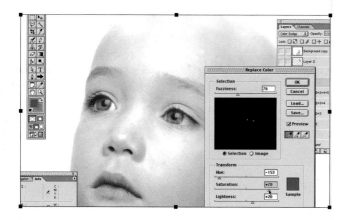

You have to be careful here to preserve harmony in the colors. If the eyes are too bright, they won't look very natural.

My advice is to create a layers folder for each of these stages so you can undo many steps, if necessary. Using the techniques described here, my final image was 515 MB in an 11 × 15 in. (30 × 38 cm) format, with a 300 dpi resolution.

At this point we can start correcting the color balance using Replace Color, and modifying the lighter colors to preserve the look of the iris. I chose a golden color for the eye that would contrast with the light purple background.

Once these corrections are done, it was necessary to adjust a few shadows with the Clone Stamp tool. ■

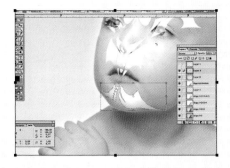

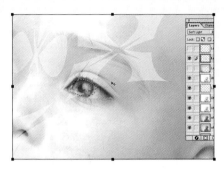

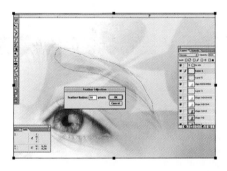

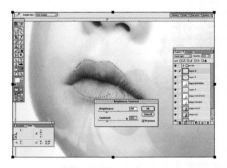

Stage 6

The tattoos

I used Illustrator to draw the tattoo pattern. Because the pattern was so complicated, it required a 3D drawing application. With a simple pattern applied to just part of a face—the cheek, for example—Photoshop would have been fine; you can get very satisfactory results using the Distort tools and Spherize filter.

Using the 3D features of Cinema 4D, I created a template of a child's face, which I oriented in the same direction as the girl's face in the photograph. I then created a specific tattooing image using the outline of the pattern as the alpha channel and applied it to the face template.

Using Cinema 4D, I created (a template **of a child's face oriented** *in the same direction as the girl's in the photo.*

At that point, I confronted two problems: the pattern didn't match the curves of the face, and because of the 3D's somewhat "frozen" appearance, the integration didn't look realistic.

I copied the drawing of the pattern onto the image, but retained only its outline. Using the Lasso to select the parts of the tattoo that weren't working right, I distorted them until they fit the shape of the face properly.

I then cleaned up the tattoo where it overlapped parts of the face, such as the eyebrows, eyes, nostrils, and mouth. Here I used the Eraser in a small size at 30% opacity. ▪

I first selected the mouth with the Lasso and created an outline with a 20-pixel feather. I lightened the tattoo over the mouth so it would be subtle, but still visible. I then did the same for the eyebrows, but instead of lightening the tattoo there, I eliminated it.

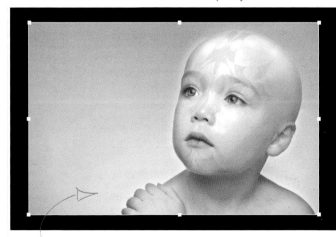

Final integration of the tattoo

Stage 7

The glasses

When I first put the glasses on the girl's face, I noticed right away that the 3D textures didn't mesh with the picture very well; the colors clashed and the contours were too "perfect."

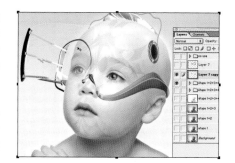

As with the tattoo, I had to first make sure the glasses perfectly fit the shape of her face. I accomplished this with the Distort tool. Once that was done, I worked on adapting the color chosen for the glasses' temple arms so it would suit the rest of the face. I copied the glasses layer and set the frame in the foreground to Difference mode with an opacity of 30%, to give texture and increase contrast.

I integrated the (the glasses in much the same way

I handled the tattooing in the preceding stage.

Working on the second layer, I used Hue/Saturation to modify the color of the glasses. The first layer would subtly reinforce the shadows.

To find suitable material for the glasses, I spent many hours copying layers and modifying their integration modes until I finally got the desired effect.

The girl's glasses would naturally cast shadows on her face, so these had to be drawn in. With the Lasso, I traced their outlines on a new layer. I then gave the selection a feather of about 30 pixels and filled it with a dark, reddish color. The layer was then placed in Multiply mode. The drop

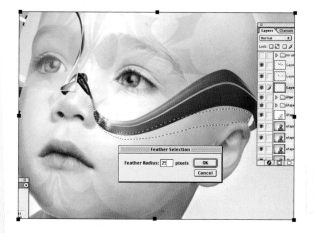

shadows fell under the side temple, the nose bridge, and the frame near the eye. I placed the shadows layer under the glasses layer so they would overlap naturally. A little common sense is all it takes to place shadows in a logical way. ▪

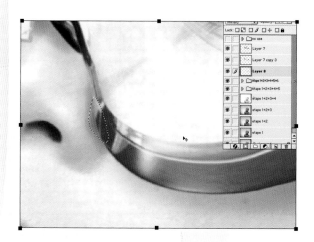

Stage 8

The screen

One way to integrate the glasses effectively was to create a slight refraction in the screen the girl is looking at. To do that, I copied the part of her face located under the glasses' screen and pasted it onto a new layer. I then used the Distort tool to enlarge this layer, and the Spherize filter to reshape it. Finally, I eliminated everything outside of the frame of the screen, using the Lasso and the backspace key. I set the layer in Brightness mode at 50%.

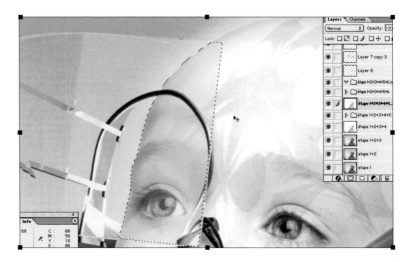

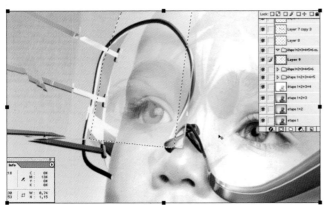

I could now integrate the material captured on the screen; it appeared as an image file I could copy and paste onto the face. Using the Distort tool, I shaped the image so it matched the size and angle of the screen. Finally, to make the projected image slightly luminous, I applied a yellowish Outer Glow and Inner Glow to the layer ▪

It was a real pleasure to finish up with this stage, because at this point it's relatively easy to achieve very satisfactory visual effects.

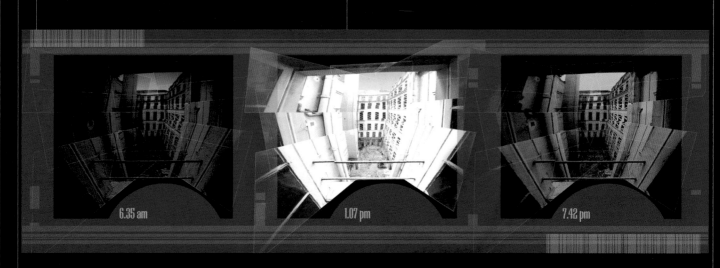

6.35 am

1.07 pm

7.42 pm

This project focuses on the changing effects of light, while recognizing that we will never be able to recreate reality exactly. Still, it sometimes happens that while retouching a photographic image, a single detail can affect the picture's entire mood or feeling. Successful retouching usually depends on carefully observing your surroundings and using common sense. Light and shadow effects have their own special characteristics. It is up to you to convey their richness and subtleties in your creations.

studio 06

TAÏ-MARC LE THANH

Shadows and Light

Hardware used
- Nikon 401 camera with 28mm Nikon lens
- Kodak Elite Chrome 400 film
- Pellicule Kodak Elite Chrome 400
- Tripod
- Epson Expression 1600 Pro scanner
- Power Mac G4 - 450 MHz dual processor, 512 MB RAM 27 GB hard drive

Software used
- Photoshop 6.0
- Illustrator 9.0

Taking the pictures   Final image

Starting with a snapshot of a condemned building's façade, I decided to create a triptych showing the view of the building at different times of day. The idea was to graphically recreate an image of ruins. What makes the resulting image distinctive is that it consists of a number of assembled photos, dictated by a purely aesthetic impulse.

The photographs were taken with a 35mm camera and ordinary film. The interest of the final image lies not its photographic quality, but in its aesthetic treatment.

The interest of the final image lies not in its photographic (quality, but *in its aesthetic treatment.*

Stage 1

Taking the pictures

With my camera mounted on a tripod, I shot the condemned building from the fourth floor of the opposite building.

I shot by instinct, without using a special panorama head. I just started with the upper left-hand corner, rotated the camera to the center, and rotated it again to the right. This produced the first row of three snapshots. I then tilted the camera down and shot a second row, and tilted it up to shoot a third.

The various snapshots were made in a (completely *instinctive way.*

To help assemble the photographs later, I chose visual landmarks by eye. That wouldn't make the assembly work any easier, but it would produce a montage that gives a fairly accurate view of the whole building. The fact that the alignment is slightly off-kilter underscores the fact that it is a graphic reconstruction.

I had the developed the photos, then I scanned them. Each photograph was then placed on a separate layer in Photoshop document. This way, I could work on them individually.

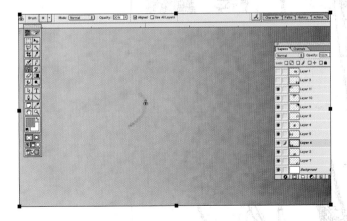

Cleaning up the photos

The photographs were spattered with little specks. To remove them, I sampled an area of material close to each speck using the Clone Stamp Tool, then covered them up. ■

Be careful in selecting which specks to eliminate, since some may contribute to the overall feeling of the final picture.

Stage 2

Brightness and contrast

The snapshots were taken with the camera on automatic exposure, and that caused some noticeable difference in brightness. The pictures in the upper row, for example, are much brighter, because the auto-exposure was reading part of the sky. All of the shots must be balanced; the difficulty lies in preserving details and colors on different parts of the walls.

The thing to do is to first establish a benchmark layer, one whose brightness level seems just right. In this case, I chose the image in the center of the lowest row of pictures.

Select the layer corresponding to the photograph that needs to be modified. Using the Replace Color function, select

the area of the wall between the windows with the Eye-dropper. Retouch the photograph until you get a color similar to the one on the benchmark layer. Do the same thing for all the layers.

Using the Color Balance function, restore the colors so they match the benchmark exactly. In this case, add some yellow and a little red to the midtones.

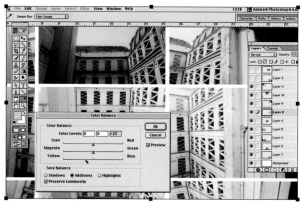

In the layer for the top center photo, the difference in brightness is such that you have to use the Brightness/Contrast function. Add a little brightness and some more contrast, and remember to use Color Balance. ■

If the lighting isn't quite the same everywhere, your work on changing the light moods in the next stages will make additional corrections necessary.

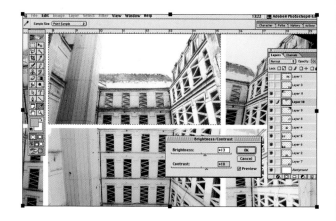

Stage 3

Assembling the pictures

Now it's time to assemble the pictures, which won't be an easy task. I used a 28mm lens, so the photos aren't like pieces in a jigsaw puzzle that can just be fitted together. For this job, we're going to need several of Photoshop's Transform commands.

Here is one possible assembly method: First assemble the center row of pictures, then the upper and lower ones. Finally, join the three rows together, while trying to distort the center one as little as possible, since it serves as a kind of horizon line.

Assembling the (photos **will prove to be** *no easy task.*

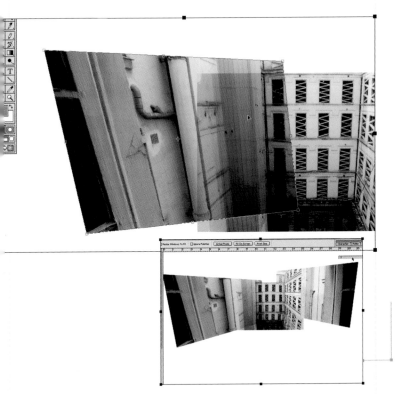

Assembling row 1

In assembling the middle row, we're going to leave the center photo the way it is. Shift the left-hand photo onto the center one while doing your best to get the various elements in the pictures to match, preferably around the vertical center line. To simplify this operation, set the upper layer in Multiply mode: that way, the two images won't be superimposed, which makes it easier to adjust their positions.

How to manipulate the left-hand photograph isn't so obvious, and it may take several tries before you get a satisfactory result. Use the Edit→Transform→Rotate command to pivot the photograph. Then use Transform→Distort and the handles on the picture's right-hand corner to stretch it so its elements match those of the center photograph.

Do the same thing for the right-hand photograph. This completes the first row.

The two other rows of pictures, the upper and lower ones, are constructed in the same way.

Stage 3

Joining the three rows

The three rows are now assembled. To join them together, merge the three layers with the three photographs that comprise each row. This gives you three layers to join.

Joining the rows is pretty tedious, and it will try your patience.

You must create a hierarchy between these three layers. I decided to use the lower layer for the foreground, because the details of the courtyard and the rubble pile were the sharpest. The middle layer would be the background, and the upper layer the middle ground.

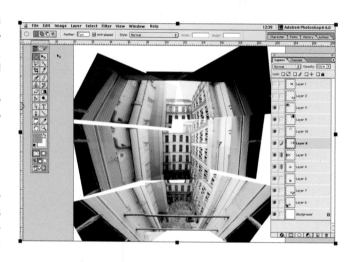

To join the three rows together, proceed the same way as before, using Transform→Distort to join the various elements so they match. This assembly is much trickier than the earlier ones, and may well take you several attempts.

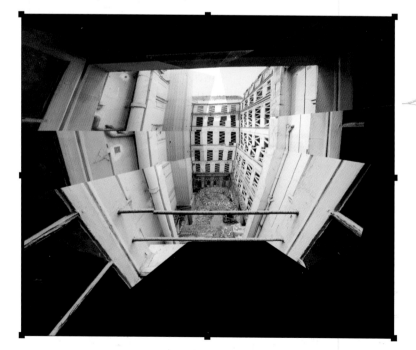

Once you have finished these operations, create a background layer and color it black, using the Eyedropper to sample a dark part of the image.

During the assembly, you will notice that it is impossible to accurately recreate the image. No matter—if that had been the goal, you could have simply taken the photograph with a fisheye lens. We are now going to work on the final assembly, turning it into an image that proudly flaunts its "reconstructed" heritage. ∎

Stage 4

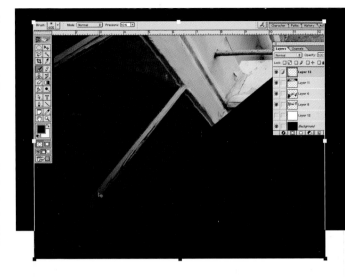

Integrating the image with the black background

Once the layers have been merged, identify the areas that aren't working well against the background—the windowpane frames, for example. Create a new layer to work on. Use the Eyedropper tool to sample the background color, and use the Airbrush tool set to a relatively wide size (200 pixels) and light opacity (30%) to paint over the window areas with a series of small strokes.

When you are satisfied with the result, merge the layers.

Accenting different parts of the image

The edges of the photographs that comprise the image are still visible, and can be accented by outlining them with a thin white line. Create a new layer and select the outline of the photos with the Lasso tool. Be careful to make the selection in several stages; if you use the Lasso to select two overlapping areas, you won't be able to select the overlap line.

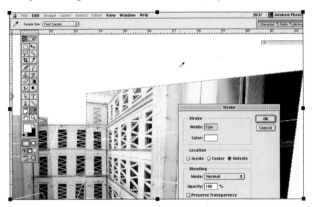

To make the job easier, create a white background layer. Once the outlining is finished, save the selection in the Paths window. Then stroke the pictures with a 2-pixel-wide line, using Layer Style➤Stroke. This setting will depend greatly on the size of the image. For a small picture, a 2-pixel outline may be too wide; for a big one, it may be too narrow.

It's now time to create the triptych itself, by copying and pasting the final image onto two new layers, and evenly spacing this series of three images. Be careful to leave the white outlines on separate layers; otherwise they might interfere with the work you're going to do on each of the three images. ▪

Stage 5

Image 1: Dawn mood

We'll start by darkening the picture to create a nighttime mood, then color part of the sky to show where the sun will soon rise.

Copy the layer of the image you are going to work on and link it to a Gradient Map fill layer in Multiply mode with 90% opacity.

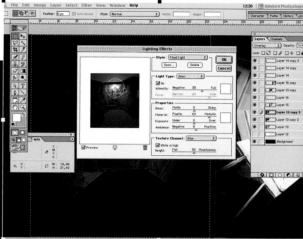

For this layer, create a gradient going from dark gray to black. Merge the two layers. This produces a dark layer, which you should set in Multiply mode at 100%. To create the effect of a glow from the sky, copy the dark layer and apply the Lighting Effects filter with the Style set to Flood Light, and the Texture Channel set to Blue with a mountainous height.

Set the resulting layer in Overlay mode at 70%. Using the Brightness/Contrast function, brighten the areas of light. This produces a dark image, slightly brightened by luminous reflections.

To work on the sky, outline the part of the sky behind the buildings with the Lasso. Create a new layer and apply a 3-pixel feather to the selection. Fill this area with very light blue. Lock the transparent pixels on the layer. To make the sky glow, use the Airbrush set to a large size (300 pixels) and very light opacity (10%), and brighten the sky with a series of touches of very pale pink.

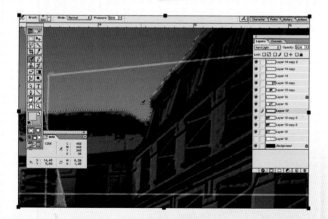

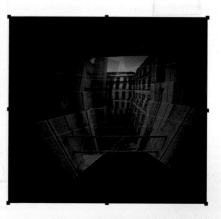

Place the resulting layer in Lighten mode at 40%. ■

To suggest the (**break of day,** you must color
the lower part of the sky

S t a g e 6

Image 2: Midday mood

There are many ways to lighten an image, of course. To keep the layer of the original image and create a new layer to work with, I superimpose the first one. That way, the resulting image always shows some trace of the underlying layer.

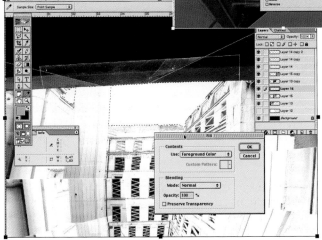

To start, copy the first image layer and connect it to a layer in Overlay mode with a gradient. Once again, choose a gradient that goes from dark gray to black. The image becomes very heavy and dark. Now merge the gradient Overlay layer with the layer of the copied image, and put this new layer in Color Burn mode. This reinforces the saturation

Like Stage 5, this stage and the next call for carefully observing the different moods of light during the day. This can be a great help in creating these images.

of the light areas of the lower layer while preserving the reduced brightness in the dark area.

Now all the image needs is a bright blue sky. Proceed as in the previous step, but replace the light blue with a much darker blue.

To brighten the sky a little, use the Airbrush tool set to a large size (600 pixels) and very light opacity (10%), and paint the sky with a series of little touches of white.

In this case, the sky layer remains in Normal mode. ■

Stage 7

Image 3: Late afternoon mood

This image must be reddish, as if lit by the setting sun. The brightness level should be dark, but not as dark as in Image 1.

As in Stages 5 and 6, copy the Image 3 layer as a Fill layer in Difference mode. When you do this, the gradient will go from blue to black.

Merge these two layers and put the result in Multiply mode at 90%, producing a reddish image. We now must take the brightness into account. To do that, copy one of the layers we created earlier for Image 2 (the one linked to the Gradient layer from gray to black). Put this layer in Overlay mode at 60%. The mood is now set; all that's missing is some nuance in the reddish glow. Using the Lasso tool, select those parts of the wall that seem less exposed to the sun, give them a 2-pixel feather, and reduce their saturation with Hue/Saturation.

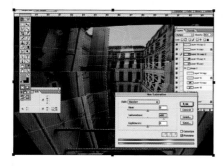

In the same way, select some exposed areas, like the corners of walls, and increase their saturation.

For the sky, proceed exactly as you did for Image 1, using a darker blue background color and a reddish orange color with the Airbrush. ▪

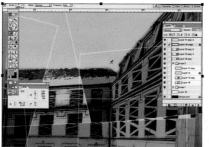

This image should look (reddish, **as if lit** *by the setting sun.*

Stage 8

The frames were built using simple geometric shapes, because there is no point in overloading the picture.

Framing the picture

We must now arrange the three finished images and create a frame for them. For this, we'll use Illustrator.

First, copy the triptych in EPS format and import it into Illustrator. The idea is to create a frame with several layers of transparency. Therefore, we have to generate as many Illustrator files as there are transparency levels, to eventually be able to place them into Photoshop.

Once finished, import them into the Photoshop image. Now arrange their layers according to the desired hierarchal level, and set them in the foreground. To make them look translucent, I set them in Difference mode: the first one is at 20%, the second at 15%, and the third at 20%.

To give **(the page** a little more life, I suggest *adding some text.*

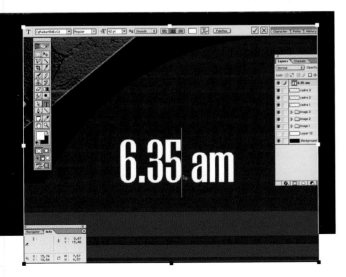

Inserting the text

This is the final touch. To give the page a little more life, I suggest adding some text. We'll use the time of day each shot was taken.

Using the Text tool, place the text under each image, being careful to align it with one of the elements of the frame. The alignment is important, as it helps structure the image. The text is in white and its layer is in Normal mode at 50%. ■

The type face must match the general mood of the image.

We had high hopes for this project, and the final result lived up to our expectations. The model's back and legs fit naturally into the framework of the squares, and the colors played off each other to create a coherent image. There are many ways one could continue working on the project: creating a shadow on the two body parts or using the tile lines to create a false perspective, which might appeal to virtual geometers . . .

studio 07

ÉRIC MAHÉ

Hardware used
- Contax G1 camera with Zeiss 45/2 lens
- Fuji Provia 100F film
- Natural and incandescent light
- Canon FS-2710 scanner
- Canon BJC-8200 printer
- Windows PC - 1.8 GHz Athlon processor, 512 MB RAM

Software used
- Photoshop 6.0

A Woman of Parts

The back   The legs   Final image

In thinking about this project, I decided I would come up with a composite image based on pictures that shared the same origin. Why such a notion? Because I think that a series of photographs taken in a particular context are easier to build into an artistic whole than a group of random images whose assemblage would seem more artificial. In this case, the two pictures—of the model's back and legs—came from the same photo session and shared the same atmosphere of the bathroom and the distinctive lighting from its large incandescent bulbs.

So how can we use parts of these two images to create a third, which would be the result of putting these digital puzzle pieces on stage? By following the same steps I take with most of my creations: create a basic document, generate a background, outline the components, put them in place, and add the finishing touches. As often happens with Photoshop, the background turns out to be the cornerstone of the work, to a point that given a good foundation—and the invaluable help of the Layer Merge mode—it becomes very easy to create a beautiful image.

A series of (photographs taken in a particular context
*are easier to build into an artistic whole
than a group of random images.*

Stage 1

The basic document

The great majority of my documents are defined by my printer's A4 page format (8.27 × 11.69 in.). I occasionally print in smaller or larger formats, but A4 is the one closest to the 8 × 12 in. photographic paper I used before converting my darkroom completely to digital.

Creating the document

Photoshop 6 only lets you create documents with a white or transparent background. However, I usually fill the background of my documents with black (which became possible as a default in Photoshop 7). I find this useful for many reasons: black "speaks" to the edges of pieces being outlined, and produces more polished results in this delicate task. A black background also does a better job of blocking the transparency of the various layers above it. This hides any imperfections or oversights in the compositions better than white does.

Having chosen size, definition, and color, we now have the basis of our document. ▪

Filling the page

In photography at least something (**real and original** is always better *than the false naturalness of a reconstruction.*

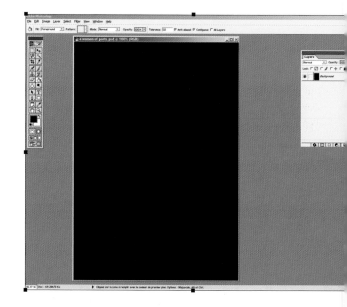

In this particular case, I chose a resolution of 500 dpi instead of the 200 or 300 dpi required for quality output from my Canon BJC-8200 printer. I first used the maximum resolution of my Canon FS-2710 scanner, which produces digital files of my slides that are about 1 × 1.4 in., at a basic resolution of 2710 dpi. Using a simple rule of three, it is easy to see that you can multiply the size of these scans by 10 (and thereby divide their definition by 10) to obtain a document ready to be printed (at 270 dpi) without having to use Photoshop's Resample Image function.

In photography at least, something real and original is always better than the false naturalness of a reconstruction. The 500 dpi resolution chosen for the base document was justified by the fact that the pieces of the image to be pasted onto it would have about half that definition, and would appear half as big on the final document. I prefer to enlarge images once they are pasted in rather than to reduce them. I always feel you gain in clarity when scaling up from small to large than the reverse—it's a matter of personal choice.

Stage 2

Creating the background

Here, I was determined to choose a background from something that already existed in the initial photographs. Despite its apparent banality, the bathroom wall lent itself perfectly to this exercise, so I copied a selection of the wall and pasted it onto the base document. You may notice that this selection doesn't precisely match the converging tile lines on the wall (which has its own perspective). This is deliberate. Not having the tile lines parallel with the edge of the document gives the creation a touch of flexibility.

The (human eye tends to look *from left to right.*

The next step was to give the background an appropriate texture. After a few tries, I settled on the Plaster filter. I selected options designed to create an asymmetrical gradient that reinforced the grout lines between the tiles. Also, I decided to make the light come from above, to match the light source in the photographs.

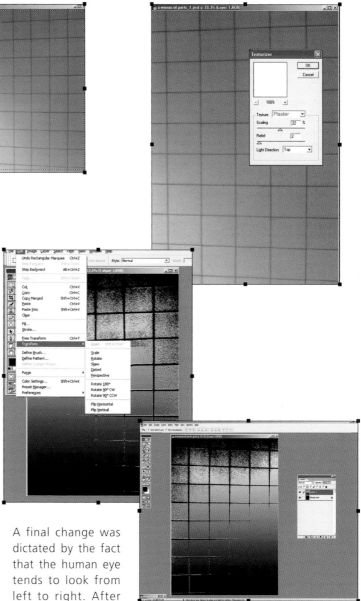

The size of the selection also determines the size of the squares visible on the background. I decided to try to select as many tiles as possible to cover the background of the composition.

To get the wall section to cover the entire base document, I brought it up and to the left and then used the Edit→Transform menu to extend it. Remember to check the Snap To option in the View menu, to make it easy to place the transformation within the document.

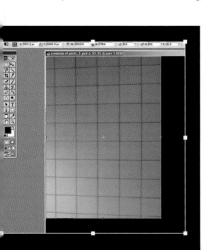

A final change was dictated by the fact that the human eye tends to look from left to right. After applying the filter, I found that the obscure parts of the gradient ran along a reverse diagonal line that might make the image hard to read. So I flipped it with the Edit→Transform→Flip Horizontal command. ■

Stage 3

Outlining the back

In Photoshop, there are many ways to outline an element in an image. I wanted to isolate the model's back from the wall, so my first instinct was to look at the layers to see if their respective contrasts had created any spontaneous masks. Alas, this wasn't the case—although the blue layer was somewhat more usable than the red and green ones.

Tools like the Magnetic Lasso or the Pen produce excellent results in outlining, but in this case they weren't well suited to the clean line of the back's contours.

The result of the selection

The (**Magic Wand**
lives up to its name.

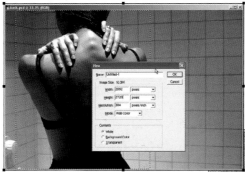

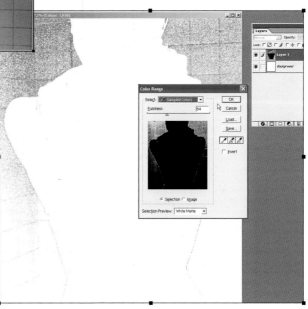

I chose another method, which would probably work in many other cases. The first step was to isolate the back as much as possible from the other parts of the image. A very tight rectangular selection lets you execute this operation. Copy the selection, go to the File menu, and select New. Photoshop automatically suggests creating a document the exact size of the copied part; all you have to do is paste the selection in it.

The next step consisted of finding the right tolerance level in the Select→Color Range menu, using the Eyedropper to select the wall (the wall's color is much more even than that of the model's back). The chosen value resulted in practically no visible selection on her body.

We still have to complete this selection to make it nice and crisp, and this is where the Magic Wand lives up to its name. Set the Tolerance value to 20, and click the Add to Selection option. The idea is to get rid of all of the "ants" in the selection and to make it as smooth as possible. You can try and click as close as possible to the body, but remember that we are working on a negative selection, and we will invert it in the next stage. It isn't necessary to "hunt" everything down because using the Select→Modify→Smooth menu option with a value of 10 on the selected zone will plug any little holes that remain.

The Magic Wand in action

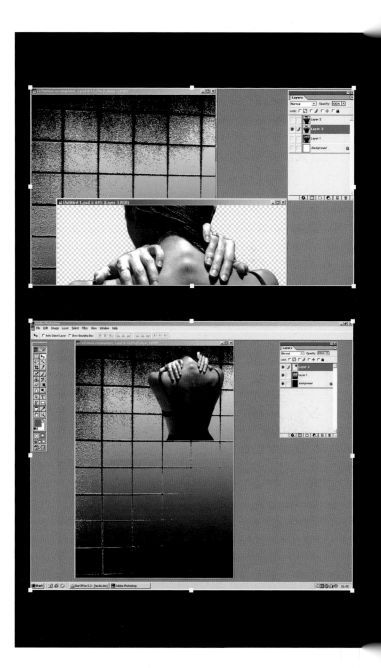

We now invert the selection and do a copy and paste to create a separate layer for the back. For some reason, the Smooth command doesn't work with a homogenous selection, so you must use the Select→Similar command to be sure to select all the pixels in the selection.

We can now return to the background while keeping the selection, and again do a copy and paste. This creates a third layer, which will be our final selection. With a simple drag and drop of this layer onto the background, the first element of the image is now ready. ∎

Stage 4

Outlining the legs

We must now choose a second element to balance the bottom of the composition. The angle formed by the model's bent knees seems perfect for filling the other lower left corner of the background. Here, the Pen tool is much better suited for the outlining. That's because I'm only interested in part of the legs, and they don't stand out as much from the background, the way the back did in the previous photograph.

The trick with the Pen tool is to use as few points as possible. I needed 11 points, which I adjusted along the contours, thanks to the anchoring point handles. The outline is then turned into a selection, and smoothed with a factor of 10 pixels.

A copy-paste operation produced a layer of this selection, which I then dragged and dropped into the document. ■

Here's another advantage of a (**black background.** When you zoom in on the two images, it helps you to better judge the quality of your outlining

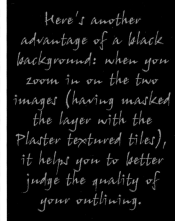

Here's another advantage of a black background: when you zoom in on the two images (having masked the layer with the Plaster textured tiles), it helps you to better judge the quality of your outlining.

Stage 5

Preparing the back

We now need to adapt the back so it fits the image's aesthetic balance. Manually resizing it should make the image big enough to stand out, and increasing the gamma level ensures that it will always have optimal brightness, whatever merge mode we choose.

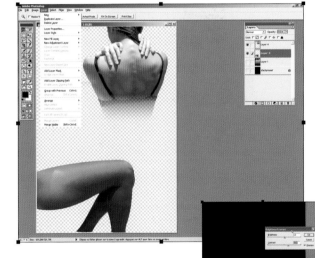

The lower back ended in an ugly straight line, which I wanted to eliminate. I created a layer mask with the back layer. Using the Gradient tool, I masked off the lower part, and the back now emerges almost naturally from the background. As a final part of this retouching, I merged the layer and its layer mask. ∎

I created a *(*layer mask **with the back layer. Using the Gradient tool,**
I masked off the lower part, and the back
now emerges almost naturally from the Background.

The choice of color is certainly the most subjective. I chose a green and greatly desaturated it, so the color would work better with the surrounding gray of the background.

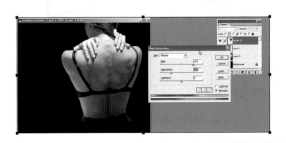

Preparing the legs

I prepared the image of the legs by following almost the same steps as before, but with different adjustment parameters. These adjustments are mainly a matter of personal choice, but I had to fiddle with the contrast to bring out the various shadows. The position of the legs fit the corner of the document naturally, so there was no need for a layer mask. In fact, the two layers could be merged to make the next stage simpler. ∎

Stage 6

Placement

I had the notion of putting the back and the legs "underneath" the background tiles, to give the impression of an old mirror or of something that had been torn, or even suggest a cage or a prison.

The first step consists of moving the tiles layer to the top of the stack. From now on this layer is the "master," giving the image its overall look. The second step was to select the grout lines, which would etch the grid pattern onto the surface of the image. The obvious choice was the Select→Color Range command, especially since setting the tolerance (to 40 in this case) let me determine the legs' visibility and also how much

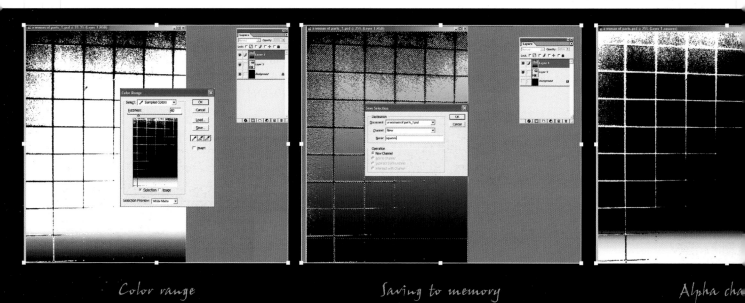

Color range   Saving to memory   Alpha cha

This may be the moment when the artistic expression is at its most delicate, or to be exact, when we must use all that the previous stages have provided as tools, elements, or fragments to be composed.

I wanted to give the impression of (an old mirror, or of something that *had been torn, or even suggest a cage or pris*

of the gradient would appear at the bottom of the image. I saved this selection as an alpha channel with the idea of joining it with another selection later. A quick glance at the alpha channel revealed that I had gotten the opposite result of what I wanted: the tile grillwork pattern was white and allowed the image underneath to show through, while the rest was masked. But that problem would be easily fixed in the next stage.

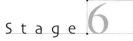

Stage 6

We are now going to use one of Photoshop's most powerful tools: calculations. The basic idea is to combine two channels to produce another channel, selection, or document by using a certain number of merge modes. At this point I'm still unable to guess what the result of a merger will be without using Preview mode. But I got what I hoped for by first creating a channel by inverting the tiles alpha channel (the simple fix to our earlier problem that I promised), then applying the Difference mode to the body channel. So the tiles are now white, the grout lines are black, and the shapes where Merge mode will be applied correspond to the back and legs. I chose the Selection option in the Result menu and—with a simple click on the creation of a layer mask on the tile layer—got a selection that turned into a linked layer mask. ■

The second selection concerned the back and legs, whose layer had to be made active. I used the Select ► Reselect command, and saved this selection in another alpha channel.

Calculations is one of (**Photoshop's**
most powerful tools.

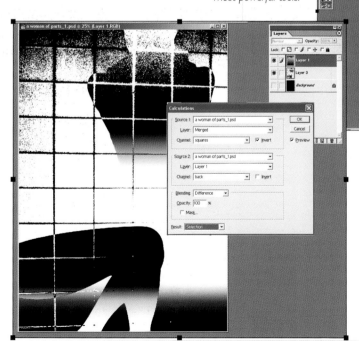

Inverted alpha channel

Linked layer mask

Reinforced by the young woman's vaguely religious gesture, the light brings an almost sacred connotation to this image. The cracks in the stone wall seem to break up the woman's face, and the picture's timeworn look is reminiscent of Michelangelo's frescoes. This creation seems closer to a piece of painted artwork, in the craftsman-like manual sense of the word, than to so-called digital work, with its connotation of extreme rigor and precision.

ODILE **PASCAL**

From Woman to Angel

Hardware used

- Canon EF camera, 50mm lens
- Fuji 400 ISO film
- One candle and one lamp
- Umax Astra 1200S scanner
- Performa 6400 - 200 MHz PowerPC, 140 MB RAM 2.4 MB hard drive
- 17-inch Pronitron monitor

Software used

- Photoshop 6.0

Taking the picture   *Overlaying the images*   *Final image*

After studying at the Beaux-Arts in Marseilles and working in filmmaking, I found a compromise between those two worlds, one in which I can put a character on stage, and then model, color, and texturize her using Photoshop. Paintings of women represent a large part of my work. Using costumes and accessories, I enjoy creating often baroque or timeless worlds, blending styles and eras, and drawing my inspiration from mythological and symbolist imagery. The resulting work, which is quite unlike traditional photography, is designed to create a fairy tale–like universe in a pictorial style close to that of the Italian Renaissance.

I decided to avoid traditional representations of angels, with their characters dressed in white, with halos and big wings, set against a background of clouds.

For this piece, (my idea was to transform the woman *into an angel.*

Stage 1

Setting up the photo

I chose a very minimal setup, using a woman named Marina as my model. Taking the full-face photograph in very dim light gave a feeling of intimacy. My goal was to render the moment like a little play; a portrait that would sum up my character's history.

The biggest part of the job would be *(integrating the two exterior textures.*

The lighting consisted of a candle and a 50-watt lamp outside the field of view, and was enough to bring out the main features of Marina's face. The objects that could be seen behind her and the arrangement of the visible space weren't important. The photograph would just be the starting point from which I would create another image, so there was no point in dwelling on the details at this stage.

When you start with a photographic setup, the tone of the image is established from the very beginning, even though many stages of transformation lie ahead. The choice of soft lighting here, for example, already set the mood—a somewhat intimate one. ▪

The orange tones of the candle flame clash with the blues of the background. Later, in Stage 4, I will suppress the dominant cold colors and spread warm yellow-orange tones over the whole picture.

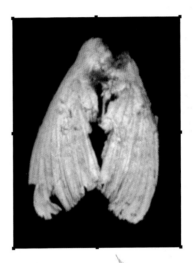

The most important thing is to have a clear idea in advance of what you want to accomplish with this iconographic foundation. I often take pictures of interesting objects or textures with a view to using them in my future work. These elements guide me when I put a mini-photographic setup together. This requires more work using the software to manipulate the picture, but it also gives me great creative freedom.

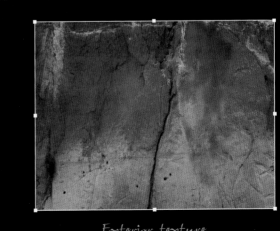

Exterior texture

Stage 2

Throughout the work in Photoshop, the light source is our guideline. The glow from the candle accentuates the quality of softness and purity in the subject's face, as seen in the Marina layer.

Initial retouching in Photoshop

I started by eliminating whatever was superfluous in the picture—the chair legs, for example—using the Clone Stamp. I first set the tool at strong opacity for most efficiency, then reduced it to 50% so as not to use a piece of the background or color twice in a row.

The glow from the candle accen

The lower-left part of the photo looked grainy, because of the carpet that was there. I softened it, using the Eyedropper to sample the carpet's original color, then very lightly covering the area with the Airbrush set to low opacity and a diameter of 60 at first, then 120.

To blur the duplication, I set (the opacity **to 33%,**
which made the blend seem more "natur

Eliminating the superfluous   Blending

I then decided to extend the brightest part of the blue background across the darkest, upper-left area, using a high Clone Stamp opacity (86%).

After smoothing the right side of the picture (which was still very dark), I used the Clone Stamp tool to eliminate the unlit candle, since it wasn't needed. I also lightened this area before I could add the butterfly wings to it, which resulted in a more visually interesting surface texture.

I duplicated the more nuanced left part of the background with the Clone Stamp, varying its opacity so as not to repeat any texture or color.

he quality of softness and purity
in the subject's face.

Now that the image was cleaner, I removed the excess red in the model's face and rebalanced the red and cyan to +18% using the Selective Color option.

Adding a background

An expanse of ochre quarry wall that I had photographed earlier would serve as the background canvas, providing the setting that had been missing from the original photograph of Marina.

After putting the Marina layer over the Background copy, I erased the layer all around the young woman, to bring out the texture's bright colors again.

Using the Eraser, I went back and forth between opacities ranging from 10 to 90%, and also varied the tool's shape (diameter from 40 to 120).

I repeated these steps until I got the desired effect. It was a long and boring job, but fortunately, I could use Edit→Undo to undo attempts that didn't pan out. ▪

uplication   *Importing the background*   *Erasing/integrating the background*

The choice of background is (**critical,** so its integration must *be done very carefully.*

Having imported the ochre texture, I placed this new layer, Ochre background, below the Marina layer. To add more nuances to the background, I copied the ochre background layer as Background copy and transformed it by lightening it, so the outline of Marina's face would later stand out against the background. This would give the picture more readability at a time when the face was overlaid with a filter on the Background copy layer beneath it.

> When you use the Clone Stamp to modify an area, you must take into account the way the light source casts shadows. To create a shadow, make an artificial gradient by varying the tool's opacity while you're stamping.

Stage 3

It was now time to merge the different elements.

Placing the wings

I chose to use some slightly velvety butterfly wings, because of their almost "vegetable" look. Once imported into Photoshop above the other layers, I had to adjust their size to fit the character. Before each wing was placed on Marina's shoulder, it had to be rotated vertically and scaled up, outlined with a 10-pixel feather, and cleaned up with the Eraser.

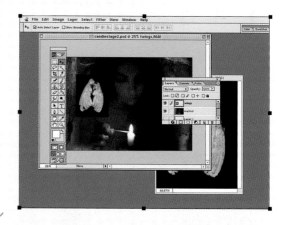

To simplify the job, and also to make it possible to make changes later, it's a good idea to copy the layers and put each wing on a separate layer.

Adding the butterfly wings (to the character

gave the scene its dreamlike aspect.

The wings were now in place, but they still needed some retouching, because the picture at this point just looked like a plain collage. Using the Eraser set to very low opacity, I softened the ends of the wings and harmonized their integration with the background.

I also changed the shape of the left wing using the Transform→Distort command, by stretching the wing to make it wider and bolder, reinforcing the effect of the light cast by the candle.

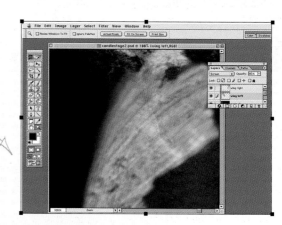

I then applied the Screen filter to each wing, reducing the opacity to 85% for one and 75% for the other. This was to avoid the kind of symmetry that always suggests "modernity." ■

The elements were now ready, but I still had to bring them together.

Stage 4

Choosing and applying colors

I repeated the operation for the wings, with a little more yellow.

At this point, I felt that the face lacked contrast, so I used the Brightness/Contrast window to remedy this, increasing contrast by +17 and cutting brightness by -9.

The effect of filters and layer stacking

To give the picture a timeworn look, almost shabby in places, I copied the Marina layer several times and applied the Texture filter with vertical Grain, varying the intensity and contrast.

Because the wings were isolated on separate layers, I had to give each of them the same treatment before erasing part of the Grain texture with the Eraser so the layers would retain their original clarity before being transformed.

To unify the different layer elements, I modified the color on the young woman and the bright blue background. First I copied, then desaturated and recolored the Marina layer, choosing 30% red and 20% yellow in the Color Balance menu. I then set the different percentages for the shadows, midtones, and highlights.

Applying texture

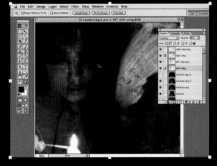

Overlaying the layers

Retouching the light source

I now combined the many stacked-up layers while applying an Overlay blending filter with lowered opacity until I got the right balance of position, color, contrast, and brightness.

The same Overlay filter was applied to the copy of the Background layer. This mix allowed the background to be seen, and brought out some graininess on the model's skin and wings. The result was harmonious, but one more detail remained to be adjusted. The various operations had lightened the candle flame to the point where it was too bright. To cool this hot spot, I outlined the flame, copied it onto a separate layer, darkened it by lowering its brightness, and placed it above the other layers. ∎

To create an image like this one, you have to get everything ready beforehand, and then not forget anything. The photographic work is important, of course, but only shooting digitally can deliver the precision required when you are superimposing images. In my opinion, what is interesting here is that the montage isn't obvious. The picture is still a "photographer's image."

studio 09

BERNARD **ROSSI**

On the Web, Rain or Shine

Hardware used
- Horseman DigiFlex camera
- Cantare Scitex digital back
- Bowens studio flash units
- Cambo studio column tripod
- Power Mac G4

Software used
- Photoshop 6
- LeafCapture 6.0

The photo setup   Preparation work   Final image

This photomontage is the result of a 2000 assignment from the newspaper *Le Figaro* for the back cover of its daily multimedia column. In the 20 months I spent illustrating this column, I tried to create montages that were humorous and a bit offbeat, on themes as varied as web sites about General de Gaulle, CD-ROMs for little girls, online adoption, and confessions on the Internet. The piece of art in this studio accompanied an article on weather web sites that were springing up. When I read a draft of the article, I thought of combining a frog—an imaginative and appealing image—and a barometer in a photograph. To make the montage amusing, I would give the frog an umbrella and set it in front of the barometer in a driving rainstorm.

The hardest part of creating (this piece was establishing which elements would get rained on—and therefore look wet—and which would not.

85

Stage 1

Creating the décor

To give a feeling of being outdoors, I took some of the stone slabs used to pave garden paths and assembled them into a décor on a table. I then took a hot-glue gun and solidly glued the barometer and the frog (without the umbrella) in place.

The choice of glue is very important: you want to be sure the elements don't move while you are taking the series of pictures—wet or dry. That way, the different photographs can be superimposed perfectly later, when creating the montage.

As a photographer, I specialize in studio pictures of objects, still lives, and people, and I've been interested in digital photography and photomontage technologies since 1994. The digital imaging chip has replaced my old-style film, and retouching software allows me to do more with my images. But I remain a photographer, and I still work at the traditional tasks of arranging settings, lighting, and composition.

Lighting the scene

To light this still life, I used two Bowens studio flash units. The rear flash, which slightly backlit the scene, was equipped with a round reflector 20 inches in diameter, and set to an output of 1500 w/s. This was the primary light.

The other flash unit, set to 1000 w/s, was equipped with a rectangular 32 × 47 in. softbox to soften the overall lighting. ■

These new tools let me be faster, (more accurate, *and more creative.*

To create the frog image I would need to assemble a décor (stones, barometer, and frog), light it, and take three series of pictures: one when the décor was still dry, a second when wet, and a third while real water was being sprinkled on it, to simulate the rain. I would then do the same thing with the umbrella, but because it is out of proportion with the other elements of the décor, I would shoot it alone against a white background, then outline it and insert it into the setting.

Stage 2

Shooting the still life

After measuring the light with a flash exposure meter to determine the lens aperture, I first photographed the décor while it was dry.

Then, without moving either the objects, lighting, camera, focus, or exposure—remember the importance of glue and stability—I dampened the whole setup with a brush, and used a spray bottle to spray the frog and the barometer with mineral water. I then photographed this "damp" scene.

Frog 1

Finally, while taking care not to move anything, my wife (and partner) sprinkled water on the décor with a watering can. I took several shots of the scene "in the rain" so I could later choose the most realistic-looking photograph.

Frog 2

A digital camera lets you check your results immediately, which saves a lot of time.

Frog 3

I now had three files that could be superimposed pixel for pixel. For the whole setup to be stable, it was important to use a very heavy tripod. ■

Stage 3

Shooting the umbrella

Photographing the umbrella had to be done separately because of the huge difference between the size of the frog (4 in.) and a normal-sized umbrella. Thanks to Photoshop, I could later reduce the umbrella's size and stick it above the frog during the montage.

I mounted the umbrella on a solid lighting tripod with a photo clamp, and shot it against a white background.

Using the watering can, I sprinkled the top of the umbrella and shot it again, this time in the falling "rain."

I took all of these photographs with a professional Scitex Cantare digital camera back equipped with a 2000 × 3000 Philips imaging chip. This single-shot back produces 18 MB RGB files. It can be adapted to different kinds of cameras:

It fits the large-format camera body I use to shoot still life. The configuration gives me a video display on my computer screen, which helps with the image's composition, framing, and focus. In this situation, the lenses are adapted to the size of the imaging chip.

Dry umbrella

Wet umbrella

The picture-taking part of this project was now finished.

Large-format Sinar camera

Horseman DigiFlex camera

It also fits a Horseman DigiFlex body with 35mm lenses, which I use to photograph people, moving objects—or in this case—falling rain. ∎

Stage 4

Preparing the layers

I then had to convert the files from the camera into Photoshop layers, since the main montage work would consist of super-imposing the pictures. I used Photoshop 6, so I opened the four files, which were in TIFF format by default. During the shoot, I named them *frog1.tif*, *frog2.tif*, *frog3.tif*, and *wet_umbrella.tif*, respectively. (See the photo captions in Stages 2 and 3.)

I imported the *frog1* file into Photoshop under the name "Work," leaving the source file intact while using it as a Photoshop layer.

At this stage of the montage, five windows were open onscreen: "frog1," "frog2," "frog3," "wet_umbrella," and "work.psd."

I began with the *frog2* photograph. I Command-clicked in the Background window of the Layers menu and chose Duplicate Layer from the pull-down menu. In a new window, I named the background *frog2*. In the pull-down menu, I chose Desti-nation Document, and selected the *work.psd* file.

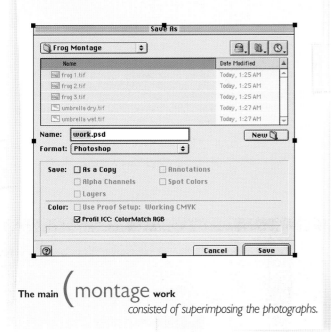

The main (**montage work**
consisted of superimposing the photographs.

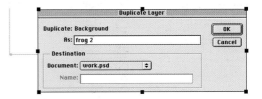

I then repeated the *frog2* operation with the next photo, thereby adding a new superimposed layer (which corre-sponded to the *frog3* photo) in the Layers menu.

This allowed me to precisely superimpose the background and the two layers—which is why it was essential to shoot all three images without moving anything.

To make it easier for me to find my way around the Lay-ers menu, I named the background *frog1*. ▦

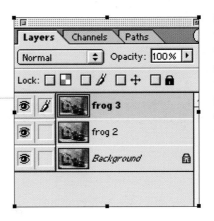

In the Layers menu of the *work.psd* file, I had the background, which corresponded to the *frog1* photo, and a su-perimposed layer that corresponded to the *frog2* photo.

S t a g e 5

Preparing the umbrella

I dragged and dropped the *wet_umbrella.tif* as an additional layer to the *work.psd* file, and renamed it Umbrella.

To sum up, in the Layers menu of this file, I now had:
- A layer that corresponded to the *frog1* photo;
- Three superimposed layers that corresponded to the *frog2*, *frog3*, and *umbrella* photos.

I could now close the four TIFF files and work on the Photoshop files.

I now had to outline the umbrella. Using the Pen tool, I created a path around the object. To record it in the Paths menu, I double-clicked Work path. It was automatically named Path 1. I then Command-clicked the Path 1 layer in the Layers palette, clicked Define a Selection in the pulldown menu, and clicked OK. I now had a selection around the umbrella.

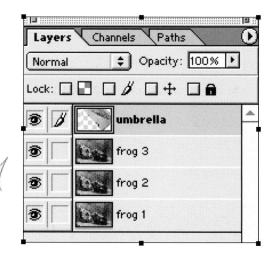

I then went to Select→Modify→Contract for the selection and entered a value of 1 pixel. While still in this menu, I set the Feather radius to 2 pixels. This allowed me to smoothly integrate the umbrella with the background.

In the Layers menu, I added a new layer mask and made the selection appear. The umbrella was now outlined. ■

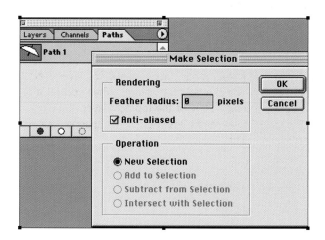

To balance the picture, I reduced the size of the umbrella, then used Transform→Rotate to adjust its angle.

Stage 6

Inserting the umbrella

I added a new layer mask to the *frog2* and *frog3* layers. This mask allowed me to erase or bring out specific parts of each of the two stacked layers by using the Brush, Eraser, and Airbrush tools.

Completing the montage

All I had to do now was to work on my three layer masks: *frog1*, *frog2*, and *Umbrella*.

Using the Airbrush, Brush, and Eraser, I brought out the areas under the umbrella that were more or less dry, as well as the droplets on the barometer, the more numerous drops falling from the umbrella, etc. My aim was to make the scene look real: caught in a downpour, the frog would be protected by the umbrella while the barometer got soaked.

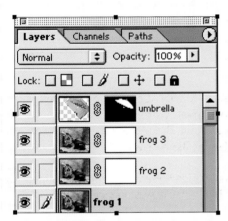
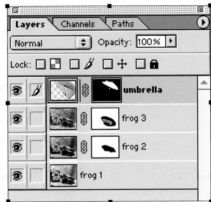
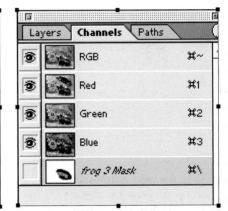

When you set a layer mask color to black, the layer is erased, which lets you see the layer beneath it. When you set it to 50% gray, you hide 50% of the topmost layer.

The use of layer masks lets you redo or change your work whenever you like.

The montage was created (in RGB mode. It would have to be converted to CMYK mode for printing.

When you select the layer mark of a layer, you can materialize it and work on it by clicking the eye of its alpha channel (same channel). ■

I wound up not using the photograph of the dry umbrella, but wanted to have it just in case.

the authors

PATRICK **COLLANDRE**

Photographer, illustrator

Patrick Collandre attended the École des Beaux-Arts in Tours, where he learned painting and model-making for cinema and photography. For the last dozen years, he has specialized in digital photography and creating photomontages. He is fascinated by imaginary landscapes and the desert, and his exhibits include *Sables émouvants*, galerie Askéo, Paris (1999), *Entre rire et larmes* (group show), *Maison des photographes*, Paris (1999), and *Chine du Sud*, Abbaye Saint-Germain, Auxerre (2002).

patrickcollandre@noos.fr • www.patrickcollandre.net

DIDIER **CRÉTÉ**

Publishing and advertising photographer

Didier Crété's work has appeared in many publications over the years. He enjoys the variety of topics he gets to tackle, and the way publishing combines freedom of expression with a demand for high-quality work. To overcome technical difficulties in creating certain images, he took an early interest in the possibilities of digital work, and first started producing photomontages with Photoshop 2.5. Today, Crété's studio is completely digital, and he considers film-based images to be part of the past.

photo@didier-crete.com • quelquesimages.com

GUILLAUME **DAVEAU**

Advertising photographer

Guillaume Daveau has been a photographer since the mid-1980s, having trained at the École Nationale Supérieure Louis Lumière. He initially concentrated on special effects for advertising and publication illustrations, but in 1994 went all digital, from the initial shoot to the final treatment of an image ready to be printed.

g.daveau@pixelavenue.com • www.pixelavenue.com

LAMIA **DHIB**

Graphic artist

After working at a variety of jobs, Lamia Dhib at 30 turned to graphic arts fulltime, which had always been her passion. More than anything, she loves manipulating images, giving them depth, character, and style. After freelancing for corporate public relations departments and independent advertising agencies, Dhib is now on staff at the Plumes de Pub agency, where she works in development.

plumes@plumes-de-pub.fr

TAÏ-MARC **LE THANH**

Freelance graphic artist

A graduate of what was then the École Municipale Supérieure d'Arts et Techniques, Taï-Marc Le Thanh has been a freelance graphic artist in Paris since 1995. His special focus is publications, book publishing, and visual communications.

tlethanh@noos.fr

ÉRIC **MAHÉ**

Image creator

A photographer and computer expert for more than twenty years, Éric Mahé only recently discovered the potential of digital methods for retouching his own images. He is now a dedicated Photoshop user, and has been fruitfully exploring digital worlds ever since.

emmahe@club-internet.fr • www.ericmahe.com

ODILE **PASCAL**

Photographer and illustrator

After studying at the Marseilles Beaux-Arts, Odile Pascal worked on movie and audiovisual productions. She is currently doing book illustration and computer-enhanced photography for posters and CD covers. She regularly displays her work at festivals and in photo galleries, including ones in Holland and Latvia.

odilepascal@yahoo.fr • http://racino.ifrance.com

BERNARD **ROSSI**

Advertising and illustration photographer

A photographer for three decades, Bernard Rossi began his career with three years of training at the CFT Gobelins school. After working as an assistant to the Paris photographer Bernard Chaudanson from 1976 to 1988, he set up his own studio. In 1993 he acquired his first Mac and in 1994 created his first digital image. Today, Rossi is still working as a photographer, but what he once captured on film is now recorded on a digital imaging sensor.

bernard.rossi@wanadoo.fr • www.quelquesimages.fr
www.bernardrossi.com

THE TRANSLATOR

WILLIAM **RODARMOR**

Translator, journalist, and editor

William Rodarmor is a French literary translator with a background in computers, law, and sailing. Of his 15 translated books, *Tamata and the Alliance*, by Bernard Moitessier, won the 1996 Lewis Galantière Prize from the American Translators Association. In the current Designer's Notebook series, Rodarmor also translated *Illustrations with Photoshop*. A freelance book editor with a fondness for European graphic novels, he lives in Berkeley, California.

rodarmor222@aol.com • http//www.editorsforum.org

studios

PATRICK **COLLANDRE** *Exotic Products*

DIDIER **CRÉTÉ** *A War of Inches*

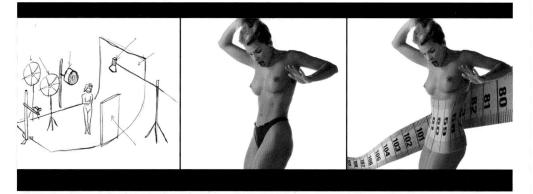

GUILLAUME **DAVEAU** *Taking Flight*

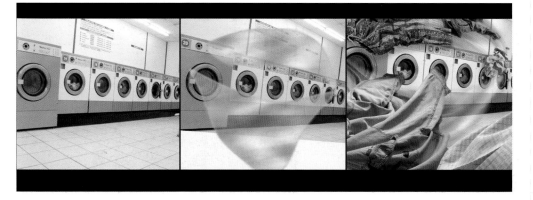

LAMIA **DHIB**   *The Perfume Woman*

TAÏ-MARC **LE THANH**   *The High-Tech Child*

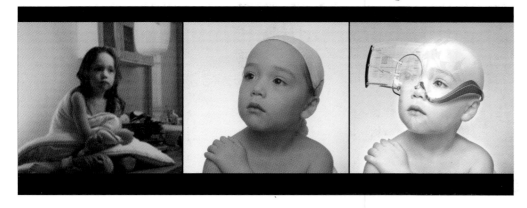

TAÏ-MARC **LE THANH**   *Shadows and Light*

ÉRIC **MAHÉ** *A Woman of Parts*

ODILE **PASCAL** *From Woman to Angel*

BERNARD **ROSSI** *On the Web, Rain or Shine*